THE Cambridge WEIGHT MAINTENANCE PROGRAMME

A guide to maintaining
your slimmer figure

Cambridge Nutrition Limited

First published in Great Britain in 1989

Published by Cambridge Nutrition Limited

ISBN 1 872151 00 0

Cambridge Nutrition Limited
69-75 Thorpe Road
NORWICH NR1 1HY

The Cambridge Weight Maintenance Programme

Congratulations! With the aid of the Cambridge Diet your efforts to lose weight have proved successful and your overweight days are now behind you. Take your time and really appreciate your success. Enjoy the satisfaction of seeing a slimmer you smiling back from the mirror in flattering clothes, with a new zest for life. Glowing with pride, you are undoubtedly determined to stay this size forever.

At the risk of dampening your high spirits, it is worth sounding the warning bells. Sadly many successful dieters find that whatever diet they follow, their weight gradually drifts upwards again. Then feelings of triumph turn into frustration. Keeping the weight off is said to be harder than losing it. ***To ensure you don't regain your excess weight, now is the time to learn new sensible eating habits that will prevent weight gain.***

Keeping the weight off won't just happen. You can't expect to stay slim by eating as much as you like, of what you like, when you like. ***Returning to your old style of eating will simply bring back your old figure.*** It is vitally important to establish a new pattern of eating as soon as you reach your target weight.

Your Cambridge Counsellor has an important role to play. Your need for extra motivation and support during weight maintenance, especially to start with, is just as great as when you were on the Cambridge Diet. Also your Counsellor will be able to supply you with Cambridge Nutrition weight maintenance products.

Finding your level

The secret of maintaining your new weight is to match the calories you eat with the amount your body uses. There is no escaping the fact that this will mean eating fewer calories than you did before you lost weight on the Cambridge Diet.

You were eating more than you needed in the first place – that's why you gained the extra weight. The main reason you now need to cut down is to avoid doing the same again! Also, a lighter body requires less energy for daily activities. Studies have shown that whatever diet is used to reduce weight, for every stone that is lost the body needs between 150 and 200 Calories less each day. So for all these reasons, gluttony is out of the question if you want to stay slim. Moderation must be the new rule!

It's all very well to say that, but what should you actually do? You certainly don't want to be on a diet for the rest of your life! Following the Cambridge Weight Maintenance Programme will help you to keep your figure without having to count every calorie and weigh every morsel of food for ever.

The programme

First comes the transitional phase (PART A), which covers the few days of eating following your time on sole source.

Then comes the main part of the Weight Maintenance Programme. The menu selections given in ***the structured eating programme (PART B)*** have been devised to help you to find out the right level of intake to keep your weight stable. You should follow this for at least a month. During this time you will ***learn through experience how much you can safely eat without putting on weight.*** The menu plans give plenty of choice, and are simple to follow. There is no calorie counting, yet you will know how many calories you are consuming each day.

Provided you keep a watch on your weight, once you have gained confidence in your ability to know how much you can eat, and where to draw the line, you can become more flexible.

Whilst you follow the structured eating plan, ***read through the informative sections grouped together under the lifestyle heading (PART C).*** Included here is the information you need to plan balanced nutritious meals for you — and all the family. There are plenty of helpful calorie cutting tips as well as practical advice on food choices, cooking techniques and portion control. Everyday needs, including budget meals and shopping are covered. There's also a section on strategies for social eating designed to help you with specific occasions, like eating out, going to the pub, choosing a take away, going on holiday, entertaining and Christmas.

Staying slim

If by any chance weight does start to creep back on then, you should resolve to do something about it immediately. ***Don't let your weight rise more than 4 pounds above your ideal weight before you do something about it. For what to do, see the very last section (PART D).*** It is easier to lose 4 pounds than it is to lose 7 pounds. And once you have half a stone or more to lose, then you've really got a battle on your hands.

For women, body weight fluctuates throughout the menstrual cycle. Some women gain as much as 5 pounds just before their period through water retention. So don't get disheartened if your weight increases at this time.

Make it a golden rule to ***weigh yourself once a week,*** at the same time of day and wearing the same clothes. It's also a good idea to ***measure yourself*** at the same time. ***Use the charts at the back of the booklet to keep a record of your weight and measurements.***

Your shape is apparent to all, but your weight is your secret. Learn to be more figure conscious. ***A full length mirror*** is essential: if you don't possess one treat yourself as a reward for losing weight. Observing your trim figure and enjoying what you see will keep you aware of any changes in your body's shape and encourage you to stay slim.

Resolve now to win the battle of the bulge — permanently — and keep your figure by following the Cambridge Weight Maintenance Programme.

Succeed with Cambridge!

THE TRANSITIONAL PHASE: Coming off sole source

First target

Coming off sole source

PART
A

First target

Before you start the weight maintenance programme, you should take your weight down to between 4 and 6 pounds below your ideal weight.

When you start to eat ordinary food again there will be a small weight gain. Don't be surprised at this, it does not mean you are putting on any fat. A proportion of your weight loss — about 4 to 6 pounds — was water. This will be replaced. (As well as this there is the extra weight of food in your gut.)

So if you haven't already done so, your first target should be to get down to below your ideal weight.

Coming off sole source

When you come off sole source it is best not to launch straight away into three meals of normal foods. ***Give your body time to adjust to eating ordinary foods again by introducing them gradually.***

For the first three days you should continue with ***three (or four) sachets of the Cambridge Diet and have a light 400 Calorie meal.*** (Choose appropriate dishes from the 400 Calorie meal suggestions given in PART B.)

Foods eaten in the first few days should be ***easy to digest,*** such as poached or scrambled eggs, grilled or poached fish or chicken (with the skin removed), served with mashed or baked potato and well cooked or puréed vegetables. Suitable desserts include low fat yogurt, egg custard made with skimmed milk, or fruit flavoured low fat fromage frais. Remember your system just isn't used to dealing with food, so give it a chance to adjust, and during the first few days avoid eating raw vegetables, high fibre cereals, and greasy or high fat foods.

Bingeing may well lead to indigestion, as well as undoing some of your hard work in losing the weight. Give yourself a chance, and get your weight maintenance off to a good start. There'll be plenty of opportunity later on for treats.

After the transitional phase, you can then move on to eating three meals of normal foods a day, but they must be smaller and less fattening than those you ate previously. This is where the structured eating plan comes in.

STRUCTURED EATING: Finding out what's right for you

PART B

The programme

This section is the key to the whole Cambridge Weight Maintenance Programme. Each day you choose from the different meal options listed. ***The programme is structured to help you find out what calorie level is right for you to maintain your target weight. This should take about a month.*** Start at the base level, 1000 Calories, and increase your calorie intake each week, as described until your weight stabilizes. The total Calories for each meal have already been worked out so there's no calorie counting — all you have to do is combine different meals according to preference to give the appropriate daily calorie level. There are no set dishes or foods. The menu selections from which you choose have been compiled from a variety of ordinary, readily available fresh and convenience foods. Some recipes have been included to increase the number of meal choices (they are given at the end of this part of the programme). The structured eating programme is very flexible, so it's easy to fit it into your lifestyle.

Each day you choose

- M *a milk allowance*
- ▲ *a breakfast*
- ● *a lunch*
- ■ *a main meal*
- ◆ *a starter or dessert*

Keeping track

Aim to weigh out all your foods during the first few weeks. This will enable you to assess your calorie intake more accurately and help familiarise yourself with the size of portions you should be eating. Also if you don't weigh your food, then you could easily end up eating more calories than you intended and undermine the whole point of this stage.

The milk allowance M is for use on breakfast cereals and in tea and coffee throughout the day. It can also be used in cooking, and recipes state whether milk is used from the allowance or not. ***Pour your daily milk allowance into a covered jug or bottle*** and keep it in the fridge – that way you can tell how much you've had each day.

In addition, once you are established on the programme, you can choose from the ★ flexi calorie options. Flexi calories include foods and drinks which can be used with a meal, to make up an extra light meal, or if you prefer for a snack. It is from the flexi calories that you can choose treats — a cake, an indulgent pud, or a couple of drinks — for special occasions.

Use the charts in PART D at the back of the booklet to keep a record of which calorie level you are on each week, and to keep track of your weight and measurements.

Drinks

You can have ***as much of any of the following drinks as you wish.*** Use sweeteners rather than sugar in drinks, and add milk from your milk allowance according to preference.

Tea	*Water*
Lemon tea	*Still or sparkling mineral water*
Coffee	*Flavoured mineral water*
De-caffeinated coffee	*Calorie free fizzy drinks*
Barley cup	*Calorie free mixers*
Herbal tea	*Calorie free squash (eg sugar free Quosh)*

Other drinks are listed in the flexi calorie section.

Getting started — the 1000 Calorie base level

For the first week, following the transitional phase, ***combine foods to give 1000 Calories a day.*** Weigh and measure yourself at the beginning of the week. Simply choose from the menu selections each day as follows.

100	100 Calories	milk allowance
150	150 Calories	breakfast
300	300 Calories	lunch
400	400 Calories	main meal
50	50 Calories	starter or dessert

Weigh and measure yourself at the end of the week. If your weight is the same, then continue on the 1000 Calorie base level for another week. ***If you have lost weight, then increase your daily Calorie intake to 1200.***

The 1200 Calorie stage

Choose foods to give 1200 Calories a day for the next week. One possible combination is given, but you can vary it, so long as the daily total is 1200. For example, you may prefer to have a 250 Calorie breakfast rather than your 100 Calorie flexi calories.

100	100 Calories	milk allowance
150	150 Calories	breakfast
300	300 Calories	lunch
400	400 Calories	main meal
150	150 Calories	starter or dessert
100	100 Calories	flexi calories

If at the end of the week your weight has stabilized, then continue at the 1200 Calorie stage. ***If you are still losing, then increase your Calories to 1500 daily.***

The 1500 Calorie stage

Follow the 1500 Calorie level for a week. One combination is given, but you may prefer to cut your flexi calories to 50, and have a 300 Calorie breakfast and a 450 Calorie lunch. The choice is yours!

150	150 Calories	milk allowance
250	250 Calories	breakfast
350	350 Calories	lunch
400	400 Calories	main meal
150	150 Calories	starter or dessert
200	200 Calories	flexi calories

If you successfully maintain your weight, then this level is right for you. If not, then either increase or decrease your calorie level.

Beyond 1500 Calories

Many people will find that they can successfully maintain their weight at the 1500 Calorie level. If you find you are still losing, then increase your intake to 1750 Calories a day.

150	150 Calories	milk allowance
300	300 Calories	breakfast
450	450 Calories	lunch
400	400 Calories	main meal
150	150 Calories	starter or dessert
300	300 Calories	flexi calories

After a week, adjust your calorie level as necessary.

Nutrition and weight maintenance

During your time on the Cambridge Diet, complete nutrition was assured despite the very low calorie level — three servings of Cambridge Diet provide 100 per cent of the recommended daily allowances for vitamins, minerals and trace elements. If you consume 1500 Calories or less a day made up from ordinary foods it is very difficult to ensure that all the necessary vitamins and minerals are available in amounts which are adequate for everyone. A study of the menu selections in this programme has shown that there is a good level of intake for most of the essential nutrients. However, to ensure ideal nutrition, it is advised that people should ***take a supplement which provides about 50 per cent of the recommended daily allowances*** of vitamins, minerals and trace elements. A pleasant and convenient way to do this is to have a Cambridge Nutrition Bar each day.

If you decide to have a Cambridge Nutrition Bar or other Cambridge product remember to adjust your calorie level accordingly. For example, on the 1000 Calorie base level, you could use one of the Cambridge products to replace breakfast or have a smaller lunch or have a 150 Calorie lunch chosen from the snack meals list in the flexi calorie section. At higher calorie levels, you could have a Cambridge product instead of a dessert or as part of your flexi calorie allowance. (Cambridge weight maintenance products can only help you to maintain your weight if you use them as part of an appropriate calorie intake.)

Once you've stabilized — the next stage

Once your weight has stabilized at a particular calorie level for at least a fortnight, then you will have discovered the calorie level that is right for you to maintain your weight.

Although you should stick to this calorie level from now on, you can afford to be a bit more flexible. You may prefer to eat less during the week, but have more at weekends. Or save up some calories for a special meal out. You can also use Cambridge products as meal replacements to help keep your calorie intake at the right level. Do whatever fits in best with your lifestyle.

Read through the lifestyle section of the Cambridge Weight Maintenance Programme (PART C). Once you've adopted the healthy lifestyle approach to what you eat, you should find that you don't need to keep such a strict count of your calories. You will gradually learn what's right for you. This isn't nearly as difficult as it sounds, after all you probably successfully maintained your (heavier) figure before you slimmed down on the Cambridge Diet! You just need time to adjust to the different amount and type of food you need to maintain your new, slimmer figure.

Continue to keep a weekly check on your weight and measurements and take immediate action if you start to gain even a few pounds. And if you do gain weight . . . turn to PART D for guidance. Remember, your Cambridge Counsellor is available to offer help and advice.

Note: Food weights and volumes are given in both metric and imperial units. The numbers have been rounded up to the nearest sensible equivalent. Please use either metric or imperial measures. (The calorie values were calculated using metric measurements.) Standard abbreviations are used, such as g for grams, tsp for teaspoons and Tbsp for tablespoons. Where food is packaged, the package quantity is given. Where wholemeal bread is indicated, 1 large slice should weigh 35 g, for example, a medium thick one from a large sliced loaf. Bread rolls should be small (50 g), unless otherwise indicated. Always use lean cuts of meat, and trim off any visible fat. Always remove poultry skin. Low fat yogurt should be used unless another type, such as diet yogurt, is specified. Calories have been rounded to the nearest 5. Because foods vary and weighing may not be exact, the calorie levels given are for guidance, and cannot be regarded as precise. For the best results, weigh your foods and follow the instructions given as closely as possible.

Milk allowances

100 Calories

100 ½ pint (300 ml) ***skimmed milk***

100 7 fl oz (200 ml) ***semi skimmed milk***

150 Calories

150 ¾ pint (450 ml) ***skimmed milk***

150 ½ pint (300 ml) ***semi skimmed milk***

Breakfasts

150 Calories

150 1 medium ***banana,*** 4½ oz (125 g) peeled weight, sliced and topped with 125 g pot ***diet yogurt***

150 ½ ***grapefruit*** and 1 ***orange,*** segmented and topped with 4 oz (100 g) ***very low fat fromage frais*** and 2 tsp ***honey***

150 2 ***Weetabix, milk*** from allowance and 1 Tbsp ***raisins***

150 1 oz (25 g) ***muesli, milk*** from allowance topped with 1 sliced ***nectarine or peach***

150 ¼ pint (150 ml) unsweetened ***orange juice;*** 1 large slice wholemeal ***toast*** with 1 tsp ***low fat spread*** and 1 tsp ***pure fruit spread***

150 1 (size 3) ***boiled egg*** with 2 ***Ryvita*** and 1 tsp ***low fat spread***

150 1 Vitbe Hi-Bran ***roll,*** 1 tsp ***low fat spread*** and 1 tsp ***marmalade***

250 Calories

250 ½ ***grapefruit*** and 1 ***orange*** segmented and topped with a 150 g pot ***natural low fat yogurt;*** 1 large slice wholemeal ***toast*** with 1 tsp ***low fat spread*** and 1 tsp ***pure fruit spread***

250 2 ***Weetabix*** with ***milk*** from allowance, topped with 3 tsp ***very low fat fromage frais;*** 1 large slice wholemeal ***toast*** with 1 tsp ***low fat spread*** and 1 tsp ***pure fruit spread***

2 large slices wholemeal ***toast*** with 2 tsp ***low fat spread*** and 1 small ***banana,*** 3 oz (75 g peeled weight) **250**

1 (size 3) ***boiled egg*** and 2 large slices wholemeal ***toast*** cut into fingers with 1 tsp ***low fat spread*** **250**

1 wholemeal ***roll*** with 1 tsp ***low fat spread*** and 2 tsp ***marmalade;*** 1 ***satsuma;*** 125 g pot ***diet yogurt*** **250**

300 Calories

1 ***orange*** segmented, 1 oz (25 g) ***Puffed Wheat*** topped with 4 oz (100 g) ***low fat natural yogurt;*** 1 large slice wholemeal ***toast*** with 1 tsp ***low fat spread*** and 1 tsp ***pure fruit spread*** **300**

1 oz (25 g) ***Puffed Wheat*** and 1 ***Weetabix*** with ***milk*** from allowance; 1 ***Vitbe Hi-Bran*** roll, 1 tsp ***low fat spread*** and 1 tsp ***pure fruit spread*** **300**

½ ***grapefruit;*** 2 (size 3) ***eggs*** scrambled with a little ***milk*** from allowance and cooked with ½ tsp ***margarine*** to grease the pan, served on 1½ large slices wholemeal ***toast*** **300**

1 oz (25 g) ***Puffed Wheat*** with 3 chopped ***dried apricots*** and ***milk*** from allowance; 1 (size 3) ***egg,*** boiled and 1 large slice wholemeal ***toast*** cut into fingers with 1 tsp ***low fat spread*** **300**

2 (size 3) ***eggs*** poached, served on 1½ large slices wholemeal ***toast*** with 1½ tsp ***low fat spread*** **300**

1 oz (25 g) ***Bran Flakes*** with ***milk*** from allowance; 2 large slices wholemeal ***toast*** with 2 tsp ***low fat spread*** topped with 2 sliced ***tomatoes***, grilled **300**

2 large slices wholemeal ***bread*** spread with 1 tsp ***margarine,*** filled with 2 oz (50 g) ***half fat edam***, cooked in a sandwich toaster or grilled **300**

1 grilled ***low fat sausage,*** 1 (size 3) poached ***egg*** and 2 grilled ***tomatoes*** with 1 large slice wholemeal ***bread*** and 1 tsp ***low fat spread*** **300**

Porridge made with 1 oz (25 g) ***oats,*** 7 fl oz (200 ml) ***milk*** from allowance and 3 tsp ***sugar;*** 1½ large slices wholemeal ***toast*** with 1½ tsp ***low fat spread*** and 1½ tsp ***pure fruit spread*** **300**

2 grilled rashers lean back ***bacon,*** trimmed of fat, with 1 (size 3) poached ***egg*** and 1 large slice wholemeal ***bread*** and 1 tsp ***low fat spread*** **300**

300 1 oz (25 g) ***Bran Flakes*** with milk from allowance; 1 toasted wholemeal ***muffin*** with 2 tsp ***low fat spread*** and 2 tsp ***pure fruit spread***

300 2 ***Vitbe Hi-Bran rolls*** with 2 tsp ***low fat spread*** and 1½ tsp ***honey***

300 2 ***Weetabix*** with ***milk*** from allowance, 4 oz (100 g) ***very low fat fromage frais*** and 1 Tbsp ***raisins;*** 1 large slice wholemeal ***bread*** and 1 tsp ***low fat spread*** and a little ***marmite***

300 1½ oz (40 g) ***Bran Flakes*** with ***milk*** from allowance, 2 Tbsp ***very low fat fromage frais,*** and 1 sliced ***banana,*** 4 oz (100 g) peeled weight; ¼ pint (150 ml) unsweetened ***orange juice***

300 2 ***Weetabix*** with ***milk*** from allowance; 1 large slice wholemeal ***bread*** and 1 tsp ***low fat spread*** and 1 tsp ***honey;*** 1 ***orange***

300 1 ***low fat sausage,*** 5 oz (150 g) ***sugar free baked beans,*** 2 grilled ***tomatoes*** and 1 large slice wholemeal ***bread*** and 1 tsp ***low fat spread***

Lunches

300 Calories

300 1 can ***calorie reduced soup*** (up to 70 Calories), with 1 wholemeal ***roll,*** 2 tsp ***low fat spread;*** 1 ***apple***

300 1 granary ***roll*** cut open, spread with 1 tsp ***low fat spread*** and filled with 1½ oz (40 g) sliced ***low fat Cheddar*** and some sliced ***cucumber;*** 1 ***satsuma***

300 1 small ***Scotch egg,*** weighing 4 oz (100 g), with a salad of ***lettuce, radish, celery, tomato, cucumber, watercress, chicory and spring onions;*** ½ a fresh ***mango***

300 1 can ***calorie reduced chicken soup*** with 2 large slices wholemeal ***toast*** spread with 2 tsp ***low fat spread;*** 1 ***apple***

300 2 large slices wholemeal ***bread*** spread with 2 tsp ***low fat spread,*** 2 tsp ***pure fruit spread*** and filled with a sliced ***banana,*** 4½ oz (125 g) peeled weight

300 2 oz (50 g) hunk wholemeal ***French bread*** cut open, filled with 2 oz (50 g) ***curd cheese,*** sliced ***tomato, watercress sprigs*** and some sliced ***cucumber;*** 1 ***orange***

1 large slice wholemeal ***bread*** with 1 tsp ***low fat spread,*** topped with shredded ***lettuce,*** 1 Tbsp ***low calorie salad cream,*** 3 oz (75 g) sliced lean ***ham,*** some sliced ***cucumber, tomato*** and ***spring onion;*** 5 stewed ***prunes*** 300

1 serving ***chicken and crunchy spinach*** (see recipe) 300

1 serving ***chicken and garlic toast*** (see recipe) 300

350 Calories

4 oz Marks and Spencer tomato, cheese and onion ***pizza,*** served with 5 oz pot ***calorie reduced coleslaw,*** and a salad of sliced ***tomato,*** some sliced ***cucumber*** and shredded ***lettuce;*** 1 ***apple*** 350

2 large slices wholemeal ***bread*** with 2 tsp ***low fat spread*** filled with 1 sliced hard boiled ***egg*** and 2 tsp ***low calorie mayonnaise;*** 1 ***pear*** 350

2 large slices wholemeal ***toast*** topped with 5 oz (150 g) ***sugar free baked beans*** and 1 oz (25 g) grated ***low fat Cheddar;*** 1 ***orange*** 350

4 oz pot ***cottage cheese and chives,*** with 1 large grated ***carrot,*** 1 sliced ***tomato,*** 1 ***celery*** stalk, and 1 wholemeal mini ***pitta bread;*** 3 oz (75 g) ***grapes*** 350

2 large slices wholemeal ***toast*** topped with 2 oz (50 g) grated ***low fat Cheddar,*** a little chopped ***onion*** and a sliced ***tomato,*** grilled until the cheese has melted, serve with 1 tsp ***tomato and chilli relish;*** 125 g pot ***diet yogurt*** 350

450 Calories

3 oz (75 g) hunk wholemeal ***French bread*** with 2 tsp ***low fat spread,*** 1½ oz (40 g) hunk ***low fat Cheddar,*** 1 Tbsp ***picallili,*** 2 ***pickled onions,*** sliced ***tomato, lettuce*** and ***cucumber;*** 1 ***apple*** 450

1½ oz (40 g) dry weight ***wholewheat macaroni,*** cooked and stirred into 1 portion of ***low fat cheese sauce*** (see recipe), topped with 2 Tbsp wholemeal ***breadcrumbs,*** grilled and served with 2 grilled ***tomatoes;*** ½ fresh ***mango*** 450

2 large slices wholemeal ***bread*** with 2 tsp ***low fat spread,*** filled with shredded ***lettuce,*** 105 g can ***pink salmon,*** skin and bones removed and flaked, and 1 tsp ***low calorie mayonnaise;*** 1 ***pear*** and 125 g pot ***diet yogurt*** 450

450 215 g can ***ravioli in tomato sauce*** served on 2 large slices wholemeal ***toast*** and topped with 1 oz (25 g) grated ***low fat Cheddar*** with 1 grilled ***tomato;*** 1 ***apple***

450 290 g can ***cream of chicken soup,*** with 1 wholemeal ***roll*** with 1 tsp ***low fat spread*** filled with 1½ oz (40 g) ***low fat Cheddar*** and 1 ***tomato*** sliced; 1 ***orange***

450 2 large slices wholemeal ***bread*** with 2 tsp ***margarine*** filled with 2 oz (50 g) ***curd cheese,*** a sliced white ***mushroom*** and 1 Tbsp ***sweetcorn*** kernels, cooked in a sandwich toaster or grilled, served with 5 oz pot ***calorie reduced coleslaw;*** 1 ***pear***

450 1 ***low fat burger,*** grilled and served in 1 ***burger bun*** with 1 ***tomato*** sliced, and sliced ***gherkin;*** 1 ***peach*** and 150 g pot ***low fat raspberry yogurt***

450 4 oz (100 g) fillet ***smoked mackerel,*** served with Waldorf salad (mix 2 tsp ***low calorie mayonnaise*** with 2 Tbsp ***natural yogurt*** and stir in 2 chopped ***celery*** stalks, 1 chopped ***apple*** and 4 ***walnut*** halves); 1 ***nectarine***

PART B

450 2 ***rollmop herrings*** with a wedge of ***lemon,*** served with 1 slice of ***pumpernickel bread*** spread with 1 tsp ***low fat spread,*** sliced ***tomato, cucumber,*** shredded ***lettuce,*** 1 grated ***carrot*** and 1 Tbsp ***sweetcorn*** kernels; 3 oz (75 g) ***grapes***

450 2 oz (50 g) wholemeal ***French bread*** with 1 tsp ***low fat spread*** and 3 oz (75 g) ***chicken liver paté,*** 2 stalks ***celery,*** 1 sliced ***tomato,*** 1 grated ***carrot,*** a little chopped ***pepper*** and 2 ***spring onions;*** 1 ***peach***

450 8 oz (225 g) ***baked potato*** split and filled with 2 oz (50 g) ***brie cheese,*** and served with sliced iceberg ***lettuce, cress*** and 5 oz pot ***calorie reduced coleslaw;*** 2 canned ***apricot halves*** in natural juice with 2 Tbsp ***natural low fat yogurt***

450 3 large slices wholemeal ***bread*** with 3 tsp ***low fat spread*** filled with 3 oz (75 g) roast ***chicken, lettuce*** and ***cucumber;*** 2 ***satsumas***

450 2 large slices wholemeal ***bread*** with 2 tsp ***low fat spread*** filled with 4 oz (100 g) ***corned beef,*** a little ***mustard*** and a sliced ***tomato;*** 2 ***pineapple rings*** canned in natural juice

450 2 oz (50 g) wholemeal ***French bread*** with 2 tsp ***low fat spread*** and 2 oz (50 g) ***Danish blue cheese,*** 2 stalks ***celery,*** 1 sliced ***tomato,*** 2 Tbsp ***pickle,*** and 2 ***pickled onions;*** 1 ***orange***

1 mini wholemeal ***pitta bread*** with 1 serving ***kidney bean salad*** (see recipe); 1 ***apple*** 450

2 large slices wholemeal ***bread*** with 1 tsp ***margarine*** filled with 2 oz (50 g) lean ***ham,*** a little chopped ***onion*** and 1½ oz (40 g) grated ***low fat Cheddar cheese,*** cooked in a sandwich toaster or grilled and served with a side salad of ***lettuce,*** grated ***carrot, tomato*** and ***cucumber;*** 1 small ***banana,*** 3 oz (75 g) peeled weight 450

1 bran ***bap*** with 1 tsp ***low fat spread*** filled with 2 oz (50 g) grated ***red Leicester cheese*** and 1 Tbsp ***pickle;*** ½ fresh ***mango*** 450

Main meals

400 Calories

8 oz (225 g) baked ***potato,*** split and filled with 1½ oz (40 g) grated ***low fat Cheddar cheese*** and 4 oz (100 g) ***tuna*** canned in brine, drained and flaked 400

2 oz (50 g) dry weight wholewheat ***macaroni,*** cooked and topped with 1 serving ***low fat cheese sauce*** (see recipe) and served with 4 oz (100 g) whole ***green beans*** 400

5 oz (150 g) ***turkey*** breast fillet, brushed with ***chilli and garlic sauce*** and grilled, served with 7 oz (200 g) canned ***ratatouille*** and 1½ oz (40 g) dry weight cooked brown ***rice*** 400

2 ***chicken thighs,*** skinned, brushed with ***soy sauce*** and grilled, served with 4 oz (100 g) cooked ***spinach,*** 1½ oz (40 g) dry weight cooked ***brown rice,*** 2 oz (50 g) poached ***mushrooms*** and 2 Tbsp ***tomato and chilli relish*** 400

1 serving ***turkey hot pot*** (see recipe), served with 4 oz (100 g) boiled ***potatoes,*** 4 oz (100 g) ***broad beans*** and 4 oz (100 g) ***spinach*** 400

4 oz (100 g) lean ***steak,*** grilled, 4 oz (100 g) ***oven chips,*** 2 oz (50 g) ***peas,*** 2 grilled ***tomatoes,*** 2 oz (50 g) poached ***mushrooms*** 400

4 oz (100 g) lean roast ***chicken,*** 4 oz (100 g) roast ***potato,*** 4 oz (100 g) ***cabbage,*** 2 oz (50 g) ***peas,*** 1 Tbsp ***stuffing,*** 3 Tbsp thin ***gravy*** 400

400 3 grilled ***fish fingers,*** served with 6 oz (175 g) ***cauliflower*** topped with 1 serving ***low fat cheese sauce*** (see recipe) and 4 oz (100 g) whole ***green beans***

400 4 oz (100 g) grilled ***bacon steak,*** served with 4 oz (100 g) ***peas,*** 4 oz (100 g) ***oven chips*** and 5 oz (150 g) ***sugar free baked beans***

400 1 omelette made with 2 (size 3) ***eggs*** using ½ tsp ***margarine*** to grease the pan, filled with 1 oz (25 g) grated ***low fat Cheddar*** and 1 sliced button ***mushroom,*** served with 1½ oz (40 g) dry weight cooked wholewheat ***pasta*** shapes and 4 oz (100 g) ***broccoli***

400 1 serving ***lamb curry*** (see recipe), served with 1½ oz (40 g) dry weight cooked brown ***rice*** and 1 tsp ***mango chutney***

400 1 serving ***spaghetti with vegetable sauce*** (see recipe)

400 1 serving ***chicken parcels*** (see recipe), served with a 6 oz (175 g) baked ***potato*** split and topped with 1 Tbsp ***very low fat fromage frais*** and a little chopped fresh ***parsley***

PART B

400 1 serving ***kidneys with sherry*** (see recipe), served with a 6 oz (175 g) baked ***potato,*** 4 oz (100 g) whole ***green beans*** and 4 oz (100 g) ***spinach***

400 4 oz (100 g) roast ***beef,*** 4 oz (100 g) roast ***potatoes,*** 4 oz (100 g) ***cabbage,*** 2 oz (50 g) ***peas,*** 3 Tbsp thin ***gravy,*** 1 Tbsp ***horseradish sauce***

400 4 oz (100 g) cold roast ***beef, lettuce,*** some sliced ***cucumber,*** 1 sliced ***tomato,*** 1 grated ***carrot,*** 1 stalk ***celery,*** 3 ***radishes*** and a few sprigs ***watercress,*** 1 Tbsp ***low calorie salad cream,*** 6 oz (175 g) baked ***potato*** with 2 Tbsp ***very low fat fromage frais,*** chopped fresh ***chives,*** and 1 Tbsp ***horseradish sauce***

400 4 oz (100 g) boneless ***pork steak,*** trimmed of fat and grilled, served with 1½ oz (40 g) dry weight cooked brown ***rice,*** 1 ***courgette*** sliced and sautéed in 1 tsp ***oil,*** 2 oz (50 g) ***sweetcorn***

400 2 small ***lamb cutlets,*** trimmed of fat and grilled, served with 4 oz (100 g) ***potato*** mashed with 1 tsp ***low fat spread*** and ***milk*** from allowance, 4 oz (100 g) ***sugar free baked beans*** and 2 grilled ***tomatoes***

400 1 ***chicken quarter,*** skinned, brushed with ***soy sauce*** and grilled, 1½ oz (40 g) dry weight cooked ***noodles,*** 4 oz (100 g) ***beansprouts,*** 2 oz (50 g) ***peas*** and 2 oz (50 g) ***green beans***

2 *low fat sausages,* grilled, served with 6 oz (175 g) *potatoes* mashed with 1 tsp *low fat spread* and *milk* from allowance, 4 oz (100 g) whole *green beans* and a little *brown sauce* 400

8 oz (225 g) poached *haddock,* served with 8 oz (225 g) boiled *potatoes,* 6 oz (175 g) *canned tomatoes* and 2 oz (50 g) poached *mushrooms* 400

1 serving *chicken curry* (see recipe), served with 1½ oz (40 g) dry weight cooked *brown rice* and 1 tsp *mango chutney* 400

1 serving *rabbit hot pot* (see recipe), served with 4 oz (100 g) *broccoli,* 4 oz (100 g) *broad beans* and 4 oz (100 g) *Brussels sprouts* 400

1 serving *liver savoury* (see recipe), served with a 6 oz (175 g) baked *potato,* 4 oz (100 g) braised *celery* and 2 oz (50 g) poached *mushrooms* 400

6 oz (175 g) *trout* grilled, with 1 Tbsp *tartare sauce,* 6 oz (175 g) baked *potato,* topped with 1 tsp *low fat spread* and a little fresh chopped *parsley,* served with 4 oz (100 g) *broccoli* and 4 oz (100 g) *carrots* 400

4 oz (100 g) lean roast *pork,* 4 oz (100 g) boiled *potatoes,* 4 oz (100 g) braised *red cabbage,* 4 oz (100 g) *Brussels sprouts,* 2 oz (50 g) poached *mushrooms,* 1 Tbsp unsweetened *apple sauce,* 1 Tbsp *sage and onion stuffing,* 3 Tbsp thin *gravy* 400

1 serving *beef kebabs* (see recipe), served with 1½ oz (40 g) dry weight cooked brown *rice* and 1 oz (25 g) canned *sweetcorn* 400

4 oz (100 g) roast *lamb,* 5 oz (150 g) boiled *potatoes,* 4 oz (100 g) *carrots,* 4 oz (100 g) *cabbage,* 3 Tbsp thin *gravy* 400

400 Calorie dishes made with Cambridge Slim Meals

1 serving *chilli with jacket potato,* served with 6 oz (175 g) *broccoli* (see recipe) 400

1 serving *chilli pittas,* served with 4 oz (100 g) St Ivel Shape *coleslaw* (see recipe) 400

1 serving *beef curry* on *potato,* served with 4 oz (100 g) French *beans* or (frozen) *whole green beans* and 4 oz (100 g) *peas* (see recipe) 400

1 serving *fusilli Bolognese* (see recipe) 400

1 serving *courgettes Bolognese* (see recipe) 400

400 1 serving ***crunchy topped cassoulet,*** served with 4 oz (100 g) boiled ***potatoes*** (see recipe)

400 1 serving ***Mexican beans,*** served with 1 oz (25 g) dry weight cooked brown ***rice*** and a ***salad*** garnish (see recipe)

400 1 serving ***Chinese beans*** (see recipe)

Starters and desserts

Starters

50 Calories

50 Large wedge of ***melon***

50 10 fl oz (300 ml) ***consommé***

50 1 serving 50 Calorie ***soup*** (eg 295 g can Waitrose low calorie asparagus or mushroom soup, 300 ml serving Sainsbury's packet French onion or spring vegetable soup, 300 ml serving Batchelor's packet spring vegetable soup, 300 ml serving Knorr Florida spring vegetable soup, ½ serving 425 g can Baxter's cock-a-leekie soup, ½ serving 425 g can Heinz cock-a-leekie soup)

50 Tomato and onion salad — slice 2 ***tomatoes*** and top with 1 Tbsp mild chopped ***onion*** and freshly ground black ***pepper,*** garnish with 1 Tbsp chopped ***parsley*** and 4 black ***olives,*** serve with ***oil free French dressing***

50 8 oz (225 g) fresh ***aparagus***, steamed and served with 1 tsp ***low fat spread***

50 4 oz (100 g) button ***mushrooms*** cooked in enough ***tomato juice*** to cover, seasoned with 1 Tbsp ***tomato purée,*** chopped fresh ***herbs*** and a pinch ***paprika***

150 Calories

150 Prawn cocktail — arrange a bed of shredded ***lettuce*** in a glass sundae dish or on a small plate, top with 2 oz (50 g) peeled ***prawns*** and 2 Tbsp ***low calorie tomato or seafood dressing,*** serve with a 1 oz (25 g) slice wholemeal ***bread*** and a scraping of ***low fat spread***

Salad Niçoise — arrange a bed of shredded *lettuce* on a small plate and top with 1 *tomato* sliced, some chopped *onion,* 2 oz (50 g) cooked *French beans,* 2 oz (50 g) *tuna* canned in brine, drained and flaked, 1 (size 5) sliced hard boiled *egg,* 2 *anchovy* fillets and 2 black *olives,* served with *oil free French dressing* 150

1½ oz (40 g) *low fat chicken paté* — served with a 1 oz (25 g) slice of wholemeal *French bread* and a salad garnish of *lettuce, cucumber* and *cress* 150

1 serving *50 Calorie soup,* served with a 1½ oz (40 g) slice wholemeal *toast* and 1 tsp *low fat spread* (for examples of 50 Calorie soups, see the 50 Calorie starter section) 150

3 oz (75 g) *rollmop herring* served with *lettuce, cucumber* and 1 *tomato* 150

8 oz (225 g) *corn on the cob* served with 1 tsp *low fat spread* 150

Desserts

50 Calories

4 oz (100 g) stewed *apple* sweetened with *artificial sweetener* and topped with 2 Tbsp *natural yogurt* 50

1 small *banana,* 3 oz (75 g) peeled weight 50

125 g pot *diet yogurt* 50

2 canned *pineapple rings* in natural juice topped with 2 Tbsp *low fat natural yogurt* 50

1 *orange* 50

1 *apple* 50

1 *pear* 50

2 *satsumas* 50

1 *peach* 50

1 *nectarine* 50

3 oz (75 g) *grapes* 50

½ fresh *mango* 50

50 1 serving ***citrus fruit salad*** (see recipe)

50 2 oz (50 g) ***lemon sorbet***

150 Calories

150 1 ***meringue nest*** filled with ½ can ***fruit cocktail*** in fruit juice from a 250 g can, drained, topped with 2 Tbsp ***very low fat fromage frais*** and 1 Tbsp flaked ***almonds***

150 ½ can tinned ***peach*** slices in natural juice from a 411 g can, with 4 oz (100 g) seedless ***grapes*** topped with 2 Tbsp ***very low fat fromage frais***

150 1/6 portion Heinz ***apple and blackberry sponge pudding*** served with 2 Tbsp ***natural low fat yogurt***

150 Bird's Eye ***choc 'n' nut super mousse***

150 1 portion ***egg custard*** (see recipe), served with 4 oz (100 g) stewed ***apple,*** sweetened with ***artificial sweetener***

150 1 serving Bird's vanilla flavour ***sugar free Angel Delight,*** made with skimmed ***milk***, served with 1 sliced ***banana,*** 4 oz (100 g) peeled weight

150 2 oz (50 g) vanilla ***ice-cream,*** with 1 sliced ***peach*** and a few ***raspberries***

150 2 Bird's Eye ***profiteroles***

150 1 serving ***trifle*** (see recipe)

150 6 oz (175 g) stewed ***apple*** with ***liquid sweetener*** and ¼ pint (150 ml) ***custard*** made with skimmed ***milk***

150 4 oz (100 g) tinned ***plums,*** with ¼ pint (150 ml) ***custard*** made with skimmed ***milk***

150 2 canned ***pineapple rings*** in natural juice, with 2 oz (50 g) scoop vanilla ***ice-cream***

150 8 oz (225 g) ***cooking apple*** cored, filled with 2 tsp ***raisins*** and 2 tsp ***demerara sugar*** and 1 tsp ***low fat spread*** and baked in a medium oven for 30 minutes

150 1 serving poached ***pears*** (see recipe), with 4 oz (100 g) ***very low fat fromage frais***

2 ***sesame Ryvitas*** with 1 oz (25 g) ***brie or melbury cheese*** and a ***celery*** stalk 150

1 ***choc-ice*** 150

2 oz (50 g) ***curd cheese*** mixed with 1 Tbsp ***pure fruit spread,*** served on ½ fresh ***pear*** 150

1 serving ***fruit salad*** (see recipe), with 2 oz (50 g) ***low fat natural yogurt*** 150

3 ***sesame Ryvitas*** with 1 oz (25 g) ***smoked cheese*** and a stalk of ***celery*** 150

150 g pot ***low fat fruit yogurt*** 150

1 portion ***rice pudding*** (see recipe) 150

4 oz (100 g) ***raspberries*** canned in natural juice topped with 4 oz (100 g) ***very low fat fromage frais*** and 2 Tbsp toasted ***almonds*** 150

1 serving ***citrus salad*** (see recipe) with 2 oz (50 g) vanilla ***ice-cream*** 150

Cambridge Nutrition products

For the purposes of making your calorie counting simpler, count them as though they provide 150 Calories. (The actual calorie level is given on the packaging.)

150 Calories

1 chocolate covered ***Cambridge Nutrition Bar*** (from a pack of 2) 150

1 sachet sweet flavoured ***Cambridge Diet Extra,*** mixed according to instructions, with hot or cold water 150

1 ***Cambridge Meal Bar*** 150

Flexi calories

Flexi calories include foods, sweets, nibbles, beverages and alcoholic drinks. You can use your flexi calories with a meal, for example a serving of potatoes or baked beans. Alternatively use them for a snack or as an extra small meal. In general, choose from the food sections, using the sweets and alcoholic drinks as occasional treats.

Note: the serving sizes of many drinks don't provide exactly the right number of calories for our categories of flexi calories, so they have been grouped under the nearest calorie level and should be counted as such. (Where this is thé case, the actual calorie level rounded to the nearest 5 is given in brackets.)

Flexi calorie foods

100 Calories

100 1 mini wholemeal ***pitta bread*** filled with shredded ***lettuce,*** some sliced ***cucumber*** and sliced ***tomato***

100 2 ***cream crackers*** with ½ (35g) pot ***crab paste***

100 ½ oz (15 g) ***sunflower seeds***

100 1½ oz (40 g) hunk ***half fat edam*** with 1 ***tomato***

100 2 oz (50 g) ***cottage cheese with chives*** on 2 ***Ryvita***

100 1 oz (25 g) ***low fat paté*** on 2 ***Ryvita***

100 1 Mr Kipling ***French fancy***

100 1½ oz (40 g) ***raisins***

100 1 grilled ***chicken drumstick,*** skinned with 1 ***tomato, celery*** and grated ***carrot***

100 3 ***dried figs***

100 1 oz (25 g) ordinary ***Cheddar cheese***

100 1½ oz (40 g) ***half fat edam cheese***

100 1 large slice wholemeal ***bread*** with 1 tsp ***low fat spread***

100 1 mini wholemeal ***pitta bread***

100 7 oz (200 g) ***sugar free baked beans***

150 Calories

1½ oz (40 g) ***muesli*** and 2 chopped ***dried apricots*** with ***milk*** from allowance	150
150 g pot ***low fat fruit yogurt***	150
1 ***jam tart***	150
1 oz (25 g) ***cashew nuts*** or ***peanuts***	150
30 g packet mixed ***nuts and raisins***	150
28 g packet ***crisps***	150
8 oz (225 g) ***corn on the cob***	150
6 oz (175 g) boiled ***potatoes***	150
1½ oz (40 g) dry weight cooked ***rice*** or ***pasta***	150
1 wholemeal ***roll*** with 1 tsp ***low fat spread***	150
6 oz (175 g) baked ***potato***	150

200 Calories

1 wholemeal ***roll*** filled with 1 grilled rasher of streaky ***bacon,*** 1 sliced ***tomato*** and a little ***brown sauce***	200
1 wholemeal ***roll*** with 1½ tsp ***low fat spread*** and 2 tsp ***honey***	200
150 g pot ***low fat fruit yogurt*** and 1 ***orange***	200
1 ***currant bun*** with 2 tsp ***low fat spread***	200
1 wholemeal ***scone*** with 1 tsp ***low fat spread***	200
2 toasted ***crumpets*** with 2 tsp ***low fat spread***	200
1 toasted wholemeal ***muffin*** with 2 tsp ***low fat spread***	200
2 oz (50 g) wholemeal ***fruit cake***	200
2 oz (50 g) ***Swiss roll***	200
2 oz (50 g) ***cherry cake***	200
2 oz (50 g) ***carrot cake***	200
2 ***Ryvitas*** spread with 2 tsp ***low fat spread*** and topped with 1 sliced (size 3) hard boiled ***egg*** and 2 tsp ***low calorie mayonnaise***	200

200 1 large slice wholemeal ***bread*** with 1 tsp ***low fat spread*** and topped with 4 oz (100 g) ***tuna*** canned in brine, drained, and 1 sliced ***tomato***

200 4½ oz (125 g) ***oven chips***

150 Calorie snack meals

150 Calorie snack meals can be used with a Cambridge Nutrition Bar (or other Cambridge product) to give a nutritious ***300 Calorie lunch.*** By adding a 50 Calorie dessert, such as a small banana or an apple, you get a ***350 Calorie lunch.*** By adding a 150 Calorie dessert instead, such as a 150 g pot low fat fruit yogurt or a baked apple, you get a ***450 Calorie lunch***.

150 1 ***Vitbe Hi-Bran roll*** filled with 1 oz (25 g) ***prawns*** and some sliced ***cucumber***

150 2 ***Ryvita*** with a 115 g pot ***cottage cheese*** and slices of ***cucumber*** and ***celery***

150 1 large slice ***wholemeal toast*** with 1 (size 3) boiled or poached ***egg***

150 1 large slice ***wholemeal toast*** topped with 1 oz (25 g) grated ***half fat Cheddar,*** a little ***chopped onion*** and ***red pepper,*** grilled until cheese has melted

150 2 ***Ryvita*** sandwiched together with 1 oz (25 g) ***low fat Cheddar***, 1 ***tomato*** sliced, and some sliced ***cucumber***

150 1 ***wholemeal roll*** with 1 tsp ***low fat spread*** filled with shredded ***lettuce*** and sliced ***cucumber***

150 1 mini ***wholemeal pitta bread*** filled with 1 oz (25 g) grated ***half fat edam,*** shredded ***lettuce*** and some slices of ***tomato*** and ***cucumber***

Cambridge Nutrition products

Cambridge products are highly nutritious and low in fat and calories, and so are ideal foods for use during weight maintenance. They also boost your vitamin and mineral intake. For the purposes of making your calorie counting simpler, count them as though they provide 150 Calories. (The actual calorie level is given on the packaging.)

150 Calories

1 chocolate covered ***Cambridge Nutrition Bar*** (from a pack of 2)	150
1 sachet ***Cambridge Diet Extra,*** mixed according to instructions, with hot or cold water	150
1 ***Cambridge Meal Bar***	150

Treats and nibbles

Free foods

hunk ***cucumber***	★
celery stalks	★
green salad of ***lettuce, cucumber, watercress, celery*** and ***green pepper*** with ***oil free French dressing***	★

25 Calories

1 large raw ***carrot***	25
2 large ***tomatoes*** and 2 ***celery*** stalks	25
1 small ***kiwi fruit***	25
1 ***satsuma***	25
1 ***brazil nut***	25
5 ***peanuts***	25
3 ***dried apricots***	25
1 Tbsp ***raisins***	25
½ pot ***calorie reduced coleslaw,*** from a 5 oz pot	25
3 Tbsp ***natural yogurt*** or ***very low fat fromage frais*** mixed with 1 tsp ***pure fruit spread***	25
½ ***grapefruit***	25
1 ***sesame cracker***	25
1 ***rich tea finger***	25
4 large ***twiglets***	25

50 Calories

50 2 Cadbury's ***chocolate fingers***

50 1 mini ***Aero*** bar

50 ¼ Cadbury's ***Wispa*** bar

50 ½ fun size ***Marathon***

50 ½ fun size ***Mars*** Bar

50 1 finger of ***Kit-Kat***

50 ½ tube of ***Polo mints*** or ***Polo fruits***

50 2 ***Rolos***

50 ¼ Cadbury's ***Flake***

50 Fun size pack of ***Smarties***

50 125 g pot ***diet yogurt***

50 1 ***fig roll***

50 1 ***Jaffa cake***

50 1 ***ginger nut biscuit***

50 1 ***rich tea biscuit***

50 2 ***mint sweets***

50 3 ***wine gums***

50 2 small ***toffees***

Hot drinks

50 Calories

50 Sachet Carnation ***slim choc*** (40)

50 Sachet Ovaltine ***choc-o-lait*** (40)

50 Sachet Ovaltine ***choc-a-mint*** (40)

50 Sachet Ovaltine ***choc-a-mocha*** (40)

50 Sachet Ovaltine ***choc-o-nut*** (40)

50 Sachet Ovaltine ***choc-n-orange*** (40)

75 Calories

75 Sachet ***instant light ovaltine***

Soft drinks

25 Calories

¼ pint (150 ml) ***tomato juice***	25
2 glasses ***low calorie squash***	25

50 Calories

9 fl oz (250 ml) ***Piermont*** (45)	50
¼ pint (150 ml) unsweetened ***orange juice***	50
¼ pint (150 ml) unsweetened ***grapefruit juice***	50
275 ml bottle ***alcohol free lager*** (40-65)	50
¼ pint (150 ml) ***alcohol free wine*** (35-40)	50

100 Calories

¼ pint (150 ml) ***grape juice*** (90)	100
330 ml bottle ***alcohol free lager*** (60-100)	100

Alcoholic drinks

50 Calories

1 fl oz (25 ml) (pub measure) ***whisky***	50
1 fl oz (25 ml) (pub measure) ***vodka***	50
1 fl oz (25 ml) (pub measure) ***rum***	50
1 fl oz (25 ml) (pub measure) ***Bacardi***	50
1 fl oz (25 ml) (pub measure) ***brandy***	50
1 fl oz (25 ml) (pub measure) ***Malibu***	50
1 fl oz (25 ml) (pub measure) ***kirsch***	50
1 fl oz (25 ml) (pub measure) ***bezique***	50
1 fl oz (25 ml) (pub measure) ***tequila***	50
2 fl oz (50 ml) (pub measure) ***dry sherry***	50

75 Calories

75 4 fl oz (100 ml) glass ***dry wine***

75 2 fl oz (50 ml) (pub measure) ***medium sherry***

75 2 fl oz (50 ml) (pub measure) ***dry vermouth*** (65)

100 Calories

100 4 fl oz (100 ml) glass ***medium wine*** (85)

100 2 fl oz (50 ml) (pub measure) ***sweet sherry*** (85)

100 2 fl oz (50 ml) (pub measure) ***rosso vermouth*** (85)

100 2 fl oz (50 ml) (pub measure) ***bianco vermouth*** (85)

100 4 fl oz (100 ml) glass ***sweet wine*** (95)

100 4 fl oz (100 ml) glass ***sparkling wine*** (95)

100 ½ pint (300 ml) ***beer***

100 ½ pint (300 ml) ***cider***

100 ½ pint (300 ml) ***lager***

Recipes

MAIN COURSES

Beef kebabs
Chicken curry
Chicken parcels
Lamb curry
Liver savoury
Low fat cheese sauce
Kidney bean salad
Kidneys with sherry
Rabbit hot pot
Spaghetti with vegetable sauce
Turkey hot pot

CAMBRIDGE SLIM MEAL DISHES

Beef curry on a potato base
Chicken and crunchy spinach
Chicken on garlic toast
Chilli pitta
Chilli with a jacket potato
Chinese beans
Courgettes Bolognese
Crunchy topped cassoulet
Fusilli Bolognese
Mexican beans

DESSERTS

Citrus fruit salad
Egg custard
Fruit salad
Poached pears
Rice pudding
Trifle

MAIN COURSES

The main course recipes given here are all included in the menu selections. All of them make up 400 Calorie main meals except kidney bean salad which is part of a 450 Calorie lunch, and the low fat cheese sauce, which is used in several different dishes. The appropriate symbol is given with each recipe, as well as the calorie count.

Beef kebabs 400

Kebabs are a colourful meal, and stretching the meat with plenty of vegetables helps to keep the calories down.

1 serving beef kebabs provides 220 Calories; served with 1½ oz (40 g) dry weight cooked brown rice and 1 oz (25 g) canned sweetcorn it provides 400 Calories.

Serves: 4

1 lb (450 g) lean beef

1 onion

1 courgette

1 red pepper

4 oz (100 g) button mushrooms

1 clove garlic

1 Tbsp oil

1. Cut the meat into evenly sized cubes.
2. Peel the onion, wash the courgette, wash and de-seed the red pepper, and cut them into 1 inch pieces.
3. Thread the beef, onion, courgette, pepper and mushrooms alternately onto 4 kebab skewers.
4. Peel and crush the garlic and add to the oil.
5. Brush the kebabs with the flavoured oil and grill, turning regularly, until they are cooked through.

400

Chicken curry

Adding a little coconut and fromage frais gives an ordinary curry an extra dimension. The pleasing creamy taste is achieved without adding too much extra fat or many extra calories.

1 serving chicken curry provides 255 Calories; served with 1½ oz (40 g) dry weight cooked brown rice and 1 tsp mango chutney it provides 400 Calories.

Serves: 4

12 oz (350 g) cooked chicken
2 cloves garlic
1 onion
1 green pepper
1 Tbsp oil
8 oz (225 g) broad beans
14 oz (400 g) can tomatoes
2 Tbsp tomato purée
Curry powder to taste
Chicken stock
8 oz (225 g) whole green beans
2 Tbsp desiccated coconut
2 Tbsp sultanas
Salt and pepper
4 Tbsp very low fat fromage frais

1. Peel and crush the garlic, peel and slice the onion, wash and de-seed the green pepper.
2. Heat the oil and sauté the prepared vegetables for 3 to 4 minutes until softened.
3. Dice the chicken, add to the pan and cook for a further 3 to 4 minutes.
4. Add the broad beans, tomatoes, tomato purée, curry powder and enough chicken stock to just cover the contents of the pan. Bring to the boil and simmer for 30 minutes.
5. Add the whole green beans, coconut and sultanas and simmer for a further 10 minutes.
6. Just before serving, season to taste and stir in the fromage frais.

Chicken parcels

400

Cooking lean chicken meat in foil parcels keeps it moist and succulent without adding any fat, and this helps to keep the calories to a minimum.

1 serving chicken parcels provides 230 Calories; served with a 6 oz (175 g) baked potato split and topped with 1 Tbsp very low fat fromage frais and a little chopped fresh parsley it provides 400 Calories.

Serves: 4

4 chicken breasts, each weighing 6 oz (175 g), skinned and boned

4 tomatoes

1 green pepper

8 oz (225 g) button mushrooms

8 oz (225 g) celery

Salt and pepper

1 bay leaf

¼ pint (150 ml) cider or chicken stock

Chopped parsley

1 Arrange each chicken breast on a square of foil. Slice the tomatoes and arrange on top.

2 Wash, de-seed and chop the green pepper, wipe and slice the mushrooms, wash and slice the celery.

3 Put the prepared vegetables in a saucepan with the salt and pepper, bay leaf and stock. Bring to the boil and simmer for 5 minutes.

4 Remove the bay leaf, drain the vegetables, and divide between the 4 chicken pieces.

5 Wrap the foil around the chicken pieces to completely enclose them. Put them on a baking sheet and bake for 45 minutes at 350°F (180°C, Gas Mark 4).

6 Unwrap and sprinkle with chopped parsley before serving.

400

Lamb curry

As lamb is quite a fatty meat, be sure to use a lean cut of lamb to make this dish, and take care to trim off every last bit of visible fat.

1 serving lamb curry provides 260 Calories; served with 1½ oz (40 g) dry weight cooked brown rice and 1 tsp mango chutney it provides 400 Calories.

Serves: 4

12 oz (350 g) cooked lamb

1 onion

2 cloves garlic

1 carrot

1 green pepper

1 Tbsp oil

Curry powder to taste

1 apple

Vegetable stock

8 oz (225 g) peas

Salt and pepper

2 Tbsp very low fat fromage frais

1 Peel and slice the onion, peel and crush the garlic, scrape and slice the carrot, wash, de-seed and slice the green pepper.

2 Sauté the prepared vegetables in the oil for 5 minutes, until softened. Add the curry powder.

3 Cut the lamb into cubes and trim off fat. Peel, core and slice the apple. Add the lamb and apple to the pan and add enough stock to cover. Bring to the boil and simmer for 25 minutes.

4 Add the peas and cook for a further 10 minutes.

5 Just before serving season to taste and stir in the fromage frais.

Liver savoury 400

Cooking the traditional partnership of liver and bacon in a casserole rather than frying makes a tasty supper dish that all the family will enjoy. It also cuts down the calorie content, by cutting down on the fat.

1 serving liver savoury provides 240 Calories; served with a 6 oz (175 g) baked potato, 4 oz (100 g) braised celery and 2 oz (50 g) poached mushrooms it provides 400 Calories.

Serves: 4

12 oz (350 g) liver

1 onion

4 oz (100 g) wholemeal breadcrumbs

Seasoning

1 Tbsp chopped parsley

Pinch dried mixed herbs

2 rashers lean back bacon

1 Wash and slice the liver. Peel and finely chop the onion. Mix the breadcrumbs with the onion, seasoning, parsley and herbs.

2 Put the liver in an ovenproof dish and add enough cold water to come half way up. Sprinkle the breadcrumb mixture on top.

3 Trim the bacon of fat and roughly chop. Arrange on top of the breadcrumb mixture.

4 Bake for 45 minutes at 350°F (180°C, Gas Mark 4).

Low fat cheese sauce

Cheese sauce is an essential part of many family dishes and makes a tasty accompaniment to many meals. However, made in the traditional way with whole milk and full fat cheese, it is high in calories. Yet cheese sauce is highly nutritious, being rich in protein, B vitamins, calcium and zinc. Making it with skimmed milk and half fat Cheddar with a little grated parmesan to give an extra cheesy flavour, cuts the calories to a more acceptable level. Low fat cheese sauce is used to make the macaroni cheese and cauliflower cheese dishes included in the 400 Calories main meal list.

1 portion of low fat cheese sauce provides 210 Calories.

Serves: 4

1 pint (600 ml) skimmed milk
1½ oz (40 g) butter
1½ oz (40 g) flour
1 oz (25 g) low fat Cheddar
4 Tbsp grated parmesan
Salt and pepper

1 Melt the butter in a saucepan and stir in the flour to form a smooth paste.

2 Off the heat, beat in the milk a little at a time, making sure there are no lumps before adding more milk. When about half the milk is worked in pour in the remainder.

3 Bring to the boil, stirring constantly until the sauce has thickened.

4 Grate the Cheddar and add with the parmesan to the sauce.

5 Season to taste.

Kidney bean salad 450

Red kidney beans are rich in fibre, protein, starchy carbohydrate, vitamins and minerals. They are relatively low in calories yet are very filling, making them a good food for the weight conscious. Combined with other ingredients they make a satisfying salad that is quick and easy to prepare.

1 serving provides 310 Calories; served with 1 mini pitta bread followed by an apple, it provides 450 Calories.

Serves: 1

6 oz (175 g) can red kidney beans

1 grilled low fat sausage

¼ green pepper

1 spring onion

1 stalk celery

1 tsp oil

1 tsp vinegar

Pinch dried mixed herbs

Salt and pepper

1 Rinse and drain the red kidney beans and put into a bowl.
2 Slice the sausage and add to the bowl.
3 Wash and de-seed the green pepper, trim and slice the spring onion, wash and slice the celery. Add to the bowl.
4 Mix the oil, vinegar, herbs and seasoning together.
5 Pour over the salad and toss before serving.

400

Kidneys with sherry

A little dry sherry adds extra flavour and interest to this dish, without adding too many extra calories. Kidney is a highly nutritious food. It is ideal for the weight conscious since it is low in fat and calories, and rich in vitamins and minerals.

1 serving kidneys with sherry provides 200 Calories; served with a 6 oz (175 g) baked potato, 4 oz (100 g) whole green beans and 4 oz (100 g) spinach it provides 400 Calories.

Serves: 4

4 lamb's kidneys

1 onion

2 cloves garlic

2 Tbsp oil

2 Tbsp seasoned flour

Chicken stock

Pinch dried mixed herbs

1 Tbsp tomato purée

1 bay leaf

8 oz (225 g) mushrooms

6 Tbsp dry sherry

Chopped parsley

1 Peel and slice the onion, peel and crush the garlic.

2 Sauté the onion and garlic in the oil for 5 minutes.

3 Wash the kidneys, slice and dip in the seasoned flour.

4 Add to the pan and cook for 5 minutes until sealed.

5 Pour in enough chicken stock to cover the pan contents, add the mixed herbs, tomato purée and bay leaf.

6 Bring to the boil and simmer for 15 minutes.

7 Wipe and slice the mushrooms. Add to the pan with the sherry.

8 Cook for a further 10 minutes. Remove the bay leaf before serving and garnish with chopped parsley.

Rabbit hot pot 400

This is an economical and easy meal to prepare. Rabbit is a low fat meat, and in this recipe it is cooked without any added fat which helps to keep the calories down. A layer of potatoes makes the dish more substantial.

1 serving rabbit hot pot provides 300 Calories; served with 4 oz (100 g) broccoli, 4 oz (100 g) broad beans and 4 oz (100 g) Brussels sprouts it provides 400 Calories.

Serves: 4

1 lb (450 g) cubed rabbit meat

1 Tbsp seasoned flour

2 onions

2 stalks celery

1 carrot

1 green pepper

¾ pint (450 ml) tomato juice

1¼ lb (575 g) potatoes

1. Dip the meat in the seasoned flour, peel and slice the onions, wash and slice the celery, scrape and slice the carrot, wash, de-seed and slice the green pepper.
2. Layer the meat and prepared vegetables in an ovenproof dish.
3. Pour over enough tomato juice to come half way up the meat and vegetable layers.
4. Scrub and slice the potatoes and arrange on top of the meat and vegetables.
5. Bake for 2 hours at 350°F (180°C, Gas Mark 4).

400 *Spaghetti with vegetable sauce*

The sauce is economical, high in fibre, packed with nutrients and very tasty.

1 serving spaghetti with vegetable sauce provides 400 Calories.

Serves: 4

1 onion

1 carrot

1 celery stalk

2-3 cloves garlic

1 Tbsp oil

14 oz (400 g) can tomatoes

Pinch dried mixed herbs

Pinch dried oregano

1 Tbsp tomato purée

4 oz (100 g) red lentils

¾ pint (450 ml) vegetable stock

8 oz (225 g) wholewheat spaghetti

4 oz (100 g) mushrooms

Salt and pepper

8 Tbsp grated parmesan cheese

1 Peel and chop the onion, wash and grate the carrot, wash and dice the celery stalk, peel and crush the garlic.

2 Sauté the onion, celery and garlic in the oil for 5 minutes, until softened. Add the tomatoes, mixed herbs, oregano, tomato purée and lentils and cook for a further 5 minutes.

3 Add the vegetable stock, bring to the boil and simmer for 30 minutes, stirring occasionally.

4 Cook the spaghetti in plenty of boiling water according to the instructions on the pack.

5 Wash and slice the mushrooms and add to the sauce for the last 10 minutes of cooking. Season to taste.

6 Serve the spaghetti topped with the sauce and each portion sprinkled with 2 Tbsp grated parmesan.

Turkey hot pot

400

Not only is turkey fillet an economical buy, it is very low in fat which means it is also low in calories. Cooked in this way with layers of vegetables and no added fat it makes a delicious low calorie supper dish.

1 serving turkey hot pot provides 240 Calories; served with 4 oz (100 g) boiled potatoes, 4 oz (100 g) broad beans and 4 oz (100 g) spinach it provides 400 Calories.

Serves: 4

1 lb (450 g) turkey fillet

1 Tbsp seasoned flour

1 carrot

1 onion

1 turnip

2 stalks celery

Pinch dried mixed herbs

1 lb (450 g) potatoes

1 Wash and slice the turkey and dip in the seasoned flour. Peel and slice the carrot, onion and turnip. Wash and slice the celery.

2 Layer the turkey and vegetables in a casserole dish, sprinkle with mixed herbs, and add enough water to barely cover.

3 Scrub and slice the potatoes and arrange on top of the casserole.

4 Bake for 45 minutes at 350°F (180°C, Gas Mark 4).

CAMBRIDGE SLIM MEAL DISHES

Cambridge Slim Meals are a range of convenient, packaged dishes, which when cooked and served with rice or pasta as directed each provide a tasty 400 Calorie main course. Slim Meals are available in a choice of flavours, including Bolognese Sauce, Chicken Supreme, Chicken Curry, Beef Curry, Chilli con Carne and Vegetarian Bean Feast. Slim Meals are economical and are available in single serving sachets. The recipes are designed to offer further variety. Each recipe serves one person, but for a convenient and tasty family meal, simply multiply the quantities.

All the recipes given are included in the menu selection as 400 Calorie main meals, except chicken and crunchy spinach, and chicken on garlic toast which are both 300 Calorie lunch dishes. Each recipe is marked with the appropriate symbol.

Cambridge Slim Meals, like other Cambridge weight maintenance products, are available exclusively from Cambridge Counsellors.

400

Beef curry on a potato base

1 serving of beef curry on a potato base with beans and peas provides 400 Calories.

Serves: 1

1 Cambridge Beef Curry Slim Meal
6 oz (175 g) potato, peeled and chopped
1 tsp sunflower margarine
4 oz (100 g) French beans or (frozen) whole green beans
4 oz (100 g) peas

1 Boil the potato until cooked. Drain. Cook the Beef Curry Slim Meal as directed on the packet. Cook the beans and peas.

2 Mash the potato with the margarine. Put the mashed potato on a non-stick baking tray and pat down to form a cake. Cook either under the grill or in a hot oven until light golden in colour.

3 Pile the beef curry on top of the browned potato. Serve with beans and peas.

Chicken and crunchy spinach

300

1 serving chicken and crunchy spinach provides 300 Calories.

Serves: 1

1 Cambridge Chicken Supreme Slim Meal

2 oz (50 g) frozen sweetcorn

6 oz (175 g) frozen spinach

1½ tsp sesame seeds

Black pepper

1 Cook the Chicken Supreme Slim Meal as directed on the packet. Add the sweetcorn 5 to 6 minutes before the end of the cooking time.

2 Cook the spinach as directed, drain well. Add the sesame seeds and black pepper and stir well.

3 Put the spinach on a plate and top with the chicken mixture.

Chicken on garlic toast

300

1 serving of chicken on garlic toast provides 300 Calories.

Serves: 1

1 Cambridge Chicken Supreme Slim Meal

1½ large slices wholemeal bread

1 clove garlic, peeled

Black pepper

Chopped fresh herbs (optional)

1 tomato

Salad garnish

1 Cook the Chicken Supreme Slim Meal as directed on the pack.

2 Toast the bread on both sides, then rub with the garlic.

3 Put the toast on a heatproof plate and cover with the cooked chicken mixture, sprinkle with black pepper and fresh chopped herbs (optional). Grill.

4 Serve with tomato and salad garnish.

400

Chilli pitta

1 serving of chilli pitta with coleslaw provides 400 Calories.

Serves: 1

1 Chilli con Carne Cambridge Slim Meal

1 wholemeal pitta bread

A few lettuce leaves, shredded

1 small carrot, grated

1 tomato, sliced

Other salad vegetables, such as sliced raw mushroom, mustard and cress, alfalfa sprouts, beansprouts

4 oz (100 g) St Ivel Shape coleslaw

1 Cook the Chilli con Carne Slim Meal as directed on the packet.

2 Mix the salad vegetables.

3 Sprinkle the pitta bread with water, then put it under a pre-heated grill and heat for approximately 1½ minutes each side, until it starts to puff up.

4 Cut a slit down the long side of the pitta bread, and into the pocket you have made, put half the salad mixture. Fill with the cooked chilli and finish with the remaining salad mixture. Serve with coleslaw.

Chilli with jacket potato

400

1 serving of chilli with a jacket potato and broccoli provides 400 Calories.

Serves: 1

1 Chilli con Carne Cambridge Slim Meal

1 tsp tomato purée

8 oz (225 g) baking potato, washed and pricked

6 oz (175 g) broccoli

1 Bake potato in a hot oven for about 45 minutes, until cooked, (or microwave on full for about 10 minutes). Turn it over half way through cooking.

2 20 minutes before the potato is ready, cook the Chilli con Carne Slim Meal as directed on the packet, using 6 fl oz (175 ml) water, adding the tomato purée half way through the cooking time.

3 Cook the broccoli in boiling water or microwave.

4 Split open the potato and top with chilli sauce. Serve with broccoli.

400

Chinese beans

1 serving Chinese beans provides 400 Calories.

Serves: 1

1 Cambridge Bean Feast Slim Meal
2 oz (50 g) Chinese egg noodles
2 oz (50 g) beansprouts
¼ tsp five spice powder
Few dashes soy sauce
Black pepper
1 spring onion (optional)

1 Cook the Bean Feast Slim Meal as directed on the packet, but use less water, about 7½ fl oz (225 ml). Add the five spice powder and a dash of soy sauce.

2 Cook the Chinese noodles as directed on the pack. (Generally, add the noodles to a pan of boiling water, remove from the heat and leave to stand for 6 minutes, then drain.)

3 Cook the beansprouts in boiling water for 2 minutes, drain.

4 Toss cooked, drained noodles and beansprouts in a bowl, add a dash of soy sauce and plenty of black pepper. Top with cooked bean mixture. Garnish with spring onion (optional).

Courgettes Bolognese 400

1 serving courgettes Bolognese provides 400 Calories.

Serves: 1

1 Cambridge Bolognese Sauce Slim Meal

8 oz (225 g) courgettes

1 beef tomato

1 oz (25 g) fresh wholemeal breadcrumbs

1 oz (25 g) grated low fat hard cheese

1 Cook the Bolognese Sauce Slim Meal as directed on the packet.

2 Wash the courgettes, slice diagonally. Cook in boiling water until tender, about 6 minutes. Slice the beef tomato.

3 Place one third of the courgettes in a layer on the base of a small flameproof dish, then half the sliced tomato, followed by half the Bolognese sauce. Repeat. Finish with the remaining courgettes.

4 Mix cheese and breadcrumbs. Sprinkle over top of courgettes, and put under a pre-heated grill or in a hot oven to crisp the breadcrumbs and melt the cheese.

400

Crunchy topped cassoulet

1 serving crunchy topped cassoulet with boiled potatoes provides 400 Calories.

Serves: 1

1 Cambridge Bean Feast Slim Meal

1 oz (25 g) wholemeal bread, crumbled

½ Tbsp oats

½ Tbsp grated low fat cheese

½ tsp tomato purée

Black pepper

4 oz (100 g) new potatoes

1 Cook the Bean Feast Slim Meal as directed, but use 7½ fl oz (230 ml) water. Add tomato purée.

2 Cook potatoes.

3 Place crumbled breadcrumbs on a baking tray or sheet of foil and grill until crisp. Put them in a small plastic bag, fold over the opening and roll with a rolling pin to crush crumbs. (Alternatively grind in a food processor or food mill.)

4 Mix oats, cheese and pepper with crumbs.

5 Put cooked bean mixture in a small ovenproof dish and sprinkle the crumb mixture over the top. Brown under the grill or in a hot oven. Serve with boiled potatoes.

Fusilli Bolognese

400

1 serving fusilli Bolognese provides 400 Calories.

Serves: 1

1 Cambridge Bolognese Sauce Slim Meal

2 oz (50 g) fusilli (pasta spirals)

1 carrot, grated

Pinch dried basil

Black pepper

1 tsp tomato purée

2 tsp grated parmesan cheese

1 Cook the Bolognese Sauce Slim Meal as directed on the packet, adding the carrot, basil, pepper and tomato purée after 10 minutes.

2 Cook pasta as directed. (The flavour is best if cooked for just 10 to 12 minutes so that it still has a firm texture — 'al dente' as the Italians call it.) Drain.

3 Mix pasta with cooked Bolognese sauce. Serve, and top with parmesan.

400 *Mexican beans*

1 serving Mexican beans with brown rice provides 400 Calories.

Serves: 1

1 Cambridge Bean Feast Slim Meal

1 taco shell (these come in packs of 8, the rest will keep if wrapped in clingfilm)

½ tsp tomato purée

1 chopped tomato

2 medium sized mushrooms, cleaned and chopped

½ tsp chilli powder

1 clove garlic, chopped

1½ oz (40 g) dry weight brown rice

Dash of lemon juice

Pinch marjoram

Salad garnish

1. Cook Bean Feast Slim Meal as directed on the pack, using less water, approximately 7½ fl oz (225 ml). Add tomato purée, tomato, mushrooms, chilli powder and garlic at the beginning of cooking.
2. Cook the rice. Add a dash of lemon juice and marjoram during cooking.
3. Place taco shell on a heatproof plate, fill it with the cooked bean mixture. Grill for a few minutes to warm through.
4. Serve with boiled rice and salad garnish.

DESSERTS

The dessert recipes are all listed under the 150 Calorie desserts, although citrus fruit salad also appears as a 50 Calorie dessert (without the addition of the ice-cream). The appropriate symbol is given with each recipe.

Citrus fruit salad 50

This variation of fresh fruit salad is sharp and refreshing, and really good to eat. It contains no added sugar and is completely free of fat.

50 Calories per serving. 1 serving with 2 oz (50 g) vanilla ice-cream provides 150 Calories. 150

Serves: 4

1 grapefruit

½ ugli fruit

295 g can mandarin oranges in natural juice

Juice of 1 lime

1. Peel and divide the grapefruit and ugli fruit into segments.
2. Add to a fruit bowl with the mandarin oranges, their juice and the lime juice.
3. Chill before serving.

150 *Egg custard*

Using skimmed milk rather than whole milk saves 50 Calories per serving in this protein packed, nutritious dessert.

1 serving provides 100 Calories; served with 4 oz (100 g) stewed apple sweetened with artificial sweetener it provides 150 Calories.

Serves: 4

3 (size 3) eggs

1 pint (600 ml) skimmed milk

Pinch nutmeg

Artificial sweetener (optional)

PART B

1 Beat the eggs, and then whisk into the milk with a pinch of nutmeg and sweetener, if desired.

2 Pour into an ovenproof dish and bake for 45 minutes at 325°F (170°C, Gas Mark 3).

Fruit salad

150

With a refreshing fruity taste, and packed with vitamins and fibre, what could be a better end to a meal, or kinder to the figure than a colourful bowl of fresh fruit salad.

1 serving provides 125 Calories; served with 2 oz (50 g) natural yogurt it provides 150 Calories.

Serves: 4

1 apple

1 pear

1 orange

1 kiwi fruit

4 rings canned pineapple in natural juice

1 small melon

¼ pint (150 ml) unsweetened orange juice

1 Wash the apple and pear. Keeping them whole, core and slice into rings.

2 Peel the orange and kiwi fruit and slice into rings.

3 Layer the pineapple rings and the apple, pear, orange and kiwi slices in a fruit bowl. Pour over the pineapple juice.

4 Peel and de-seed the melon, scoop out the flesh using a melon baller.

5 Arrange on top of the sliced fruits.

6 Pour over the orange juice and chill before serving.

150 Poached pears

Provided they are not sweetened with too much sugar and served with lashings of cream, fruity puddings make a good low calorie choice. They also provide plenty of vitamins and fibre.

1 serving provides 100 Calories; served with 4 oz (100 g) very low fat fromage frais it provides 150 Calories.

Serves: 4

4 large dessert pears
½ pint (300 ml) sweet cider
1 oz (25 g) brown sugar
Pinch ground ginger
1 cinnamon stick

1 Halve the pears, peel, core and cut into slices.
2 Put the pears in a saucepan and cover with the cider. Add the sugar, ginger and cinnamon.
3 Slowly bring to simmering point and cook for 15 to 20 minutes until the pears are soft. Can be served hot or chilled and served cold.

Rice pudding 150

Making this traditional pudding with skimmed milk rather than whole milk, and topping it with sugar free jam saves at least 60 Calories per serving. It makes a nutritious and filling end to a meal.

150 Calories per serving.

Serves: 4

2 oz (50 g) pudding rice
1½ oz (40 g) sugar
1 pint (600 ml) skimmed milk
4 tsp sugar free raspberry jam

1 Wash the rice.
2 Put the rice, sugar and milk into a greased pie dish.
3 Bake slowly for 2½ hours, at 325°F (170°C, Gas Mark 3).
4 Serve topped with raspberry jam.

150 *Trifle*

Trifle is everyone's favourite, but an average serving would normally be at least 250 Calories. To keep the calories down in this recipe the custard is made with skimmed milk, and rather than adding a third layer of thick cream the trifle is decorated with a few swirls of aerosol cream.

150 Calories per serving.

Serves: 8

8 sponge fingers

213 g can blackcurrants in fruit juice

1 blackcurrant jelly

1 pint (600 ml) custard, made with skimmed milk and artificial sweetener

4 glacé cherries

1 Tbsp toasted flaked almonds

Aerosol cream

1 Arrange the sponge fingers in the bottom of a trifle dish and pour over the blackcurrants and their juice.

2 Make the jelly according to the instructions, allow to cool, pour over the sponge fingers and fruit, and leave until almost set.

3 Pour over the custard and chill.

4 Just before serving decorate with the cherries, almonds and a little aerosol cream.

LIFESTYLE:
Stay slim, eat slim

Introduction

Once you've followed the structured eating programme for about a month, and successfully kept your weight steady for at least a fortnight, you'll know how many calories you need each day to maintain your ideal weight. This section, which you should read whilst on the structured eating programme, teaches you the simple nutritional ideas which were used to create it. Once you've mastered these for yourself, you'll have even more options. Use the nutritional information in the lifestyle section to plan your eating, dipping into the menu selections for ideas whenever you like.

Other healthy lifestyle concepts, like keeping your alcohol intake down and the value of exercise are also discussed.

You will find you get most benefit from the lifestyle section, if you ***read each section several times and absorb the information before going on to the next.*** It's also helpful to re-read the information, and refresh your memory.

PART C

Keep on weighing and measuring yourself every week. Use the charts in Part D to keep a record of your progress. If you put on more than 4 pounds (other than just before your period), then take action immediately to get back to your ideal weight.

1 All about Calories

What are Calories?

Energy is essential for every bodily function, from walking and running, to keeping the heart beating, the lungs breathing, and even digesting food. The energy contained in food and the energy the body uses are both measured in Calories, or, more accurately, kilocalories. (KiloJoules is the alternative metric measure of calories, 1 Calorie or kilocalorie is equivalent to 4.2 kiloJoules.)

Calories in foods

The components in food which supply calories are fat, carbohydrate, protein and alcohol. ***The most concentrated source of calories is fat, providing 250 Calories per ounce,*** whereas protein and carbohydrate provide less than half of this, and water has none.

	Calories per ounce	*Calories per gram*
Fat	250	9
Alcohol	200	7
Protein	110	4
Carbohydrate	110	4
Water	0	0

PART C

Most foods contain varying proportions of fat, protein, carbohydrate and water. It follows then, that ***foods rich in fat, such as butter, cream and pastry, are high in calories.*** Foods that contain a lot of water, like fruit and vegetables are low in calories.

Calorie requirements

Most adult men use between 2000 and 3000 Calories a day, whereas women use between 1500 and 2500. Young, tall, and active types burn more calories than older, shorter people who lead a more sedentary lifestyle. Maintaining your weight involves eating no more calories than your body uses.

The structured eating programme is designed to help you find out the right calorie intake for you. Keep to this level and your weight will remain stable.

Keeping your calorie intake in check

Calorie intake depends on how much food you eat. The structured eating programme will have taught you the portion sizes you can safely eat. Other ways to keep calorie intake in check include cutting down on high fat foods, choosing unrefined foods (in place of refined ones), eating regular meals, and cutting down on snacks between meals.

High in fat, high in calories

Cutting back on high fat foods is the easiest way to prevent an excessive calorie intake. Fat is a concentrated source of calories and because fatty foods are not usually bulky, cutting fat calories makes little difference to the amount of food you can eat. For example, if you top a baked potato with chopped parsley and very low fat fromage frais rather than a large knob of butter, it will save calories without reducing the filling power of the meal.

HIGH FAT FOODS

Cut down on these high fat, high calorie foods.

Fatty cuts of meat

Pies and pastry

Meat products such as salami and paté

Butter, margarine, and oil

Fried foods

Salad dressings and mayonnaise

Cream

Creamy and full fat cheeses

Creamy puddings, soups and sauces

Biscuits and cakes

Nuts

Chocolate

Low calorie products

Always choose low calorie or low fat varieties of foods and drinks to help limit your overall calorie intake. In theory, it should be easier to keep trim than it was in the past. There is an increasing choice of low fat, low calorie foods available. Most packaged foods are now labelled with their calorie value, making it simple to keep a check on your calorie intake.

PUTTING THE RECORD STRAIGHT

Margarine has fewer calories than butter! Not true. They both have ***the same.*** You can save calories by using low fat spread.

Potatoes are fattening! Not true. They are ***medium calorie foods,*** and help you to satisfy your appetite (provided you cook them without extra fat!).

Anything with sugar in it is fattening! Not true. Ounce for ounce sugar has the ***same calories as protein and other carbohydrates.*** Sugar however provides ***'empty calories',*** that is calories without nutrition.

Meat is high in fat and should be avoided! Not true. Lean cuts of red meat, cooked without the addition of extra fat do not contain excessive calories. Cut off visible meat fat, and ***use less fatty cuts of meat.***

To keep your weight down cut out bread! Not true. Bread is a staple food that is high in starchy carbohydrate and helps to ***fill you up without being too high in calories.*** But don't smother it with a thick layer of butter or margarine.

SUMMARY – CALORIES

By eating more of the lower calorie foods you can eat larger meals than if you choose higher calorie foods.

- ***Cut down on high fat, high calorie foods***
- ***Use low calorie products***
- ***Read labels on packaged foods***

TOP TEN CALORIE DECEIVERS

1 ***Avocado pears*** may be fruit but they are unusually rich in oil. At 225 Calories for half a large avocado pear, it has ***five times more calories than an ordinary pear.***

2 ***Bottled low carbohydrate lager*** may appear to be low in calories, but because it is high in alcohol it is actually ***higher in calories than ordinary lager.***

3 ***Chicken*** is low in calories provided you don't eat the skin. A skinned chicken thigh has about 100 Calories, but ***eating the skin adds half as many calories again,*** putting it up to 150 Calories.

4 ***Soft cheeses*** vary in calorie content ***depending on the fat content.*** Cream cheese has 110 Calories per ounce (25 g) compared to only 20 Calories for quark; so read the labels and choose carefully.

5 ***Salads*** are low in calories, provided they are ***not smothered with mayonnaise or an oil based dressing.***

6 ***Pastry*** is very calorie costly, providing around 150 Calories per ounce (25 g). That is at least ***twice as many calories per ounce as chips.***

7 ***Salami*** is high in fat and has ***three times the number of calories as lean ham.***

8 ***Salmon is not as low in calories as other kinds of fish.*** A 4 ounce (100 g) can of pink salmon has 150 Calories and red salmon 175, compared to tuna fish in brine at 100 Calories. An 8 ounce (225 g) fresh salmon steak provides around 400 Calories, as compared to 170 Calories for cod.

9 ***Greek strained yogurt*** — don't be fooled into thinking that because it's yogurt it must be low in calories. This type is high in fat and so higher in calories than other types of yogurt, with 135 Calories per 4 ounce serving (100 g), compared to 50 Calories for low fat natural yogurt — ***that's nearly three times more.***

10 ***Carob bars*** are an alternative to chocolate, but even the unsweetened bars have as ***many calories as chocolate.***

CALORIE CUTTERS

Quantity	Usual food	Calories	Low calorie alternative	Calories	Saving
1	grilled sausage	135	grilled low fat sausage	100	35
1	grilled burger	125	grilled low fat burger	85	40
1 tsp	butter or margarine	35	low fat spread	20	15
4 oz (100 g)	baked beans	70	sugar free baked beans	55	15
4 oz (100 g)	deep fried chips	255	oven chips	200	55
small packet	crisps	140	low fat crisps	115	25
½ pint (300 ml)	soup	100	low calcrie soup	45-70	30-55
¼ pint (150 ml)	whole milk	95	skimmed milk	50	45
1 tsp	sugar	17	artificial sweetener	0	17
1 tsp	jam or marmalade	15	pure fruit spread	5	10
5.3 oz (150 g)	pot fruit yogurt	130-150	diet yogurt	50	80-100
2 oz (50 g)	paté	160	low fat paté	100	60
1 oz (25 g)	Cheddar	100	low fat Cheddar	75	25
1 oz (25 g)	cheese spread	75	low fat cheese spread	50	25
5 oz	pot coleslaw	180	calorie reduced coleslaw	55	125
1 Tbsp	mayonnaise	120	low calorie mayonnaise	45	75
1 Tbsp	salad cream	45	low calorie salad cream	25	20
1 Tbsp	French dressing	80	oil free French dressing	0	80
2 Tbsp	double cream	110	natural yogurt	15	95

2 Calorie counter

These lists give the Calorie values for typical servings of the kinds of healthy foods that form the basis of the Cambridge Weight Maintenance Programme.

Meat

Poultry with the skin removed is low in fat and calories. Although red meat tends to be higher in fat, there's no need to cut it out provided you choose lean cuts.

	Calories
4 oz (100 g) lean ***roast beef***	155
4 oz (100 g) lean ***roast lamb***	190
4 oz (100 g) lean ***roast pork***	185
4 oz (100 g) lean ***roast chicken***	145
4 oz (100 g) lean ***roast turkey***	140
4½ oz (125 g) ***pork chop***, lean only, grilled	175
2 ***lamb cutlets***, 3 oz (75 g) each, lean only, grilled	210
1 average ***low fat burger***, grilled	85
1 average ***low fat sausage***, grilled	100
4 oz (100 g) ***lean ham***	165
1 rasher of ***streaky bacon***, well grilled	50
4 oz (100 g) grilled ***gammon steak***	170
6 oz (175 g) grilled ***rump steak***	295
8 oz (225 g) ***stew***	270
1 ***chicken quarter***, skinned, baked or grilled	200
2 ***chicken thighs***, skinned, baked or grilled	200
2 ***chicken drumsticks***, skinned, baked or grilled	150
6 oz (175 g) ***turkey breast fillet***, baked or grilled	180
8 oz (225 g) ***shepherd's pie***	265
1 ***frankfurter***	80
1 ***lamb's kidney***, grilled	80
1 ***pig's kidney***, grilled	125
4 oz (100 g) grilled ***lamb's liver***	180

Fish

White fish is lower in calories than so called oily fish. Choose fish canned in brine rather than oil.

	Calories
6 oz (175 g) ***cod, haddock, whiting,*** or ***coley*** steak, steamed, baked or grilled	135
6 oz (175 g) ***fillet of plaice***, baked or grilled	160
2 ***fish fingers***, baked or grilled	100
2 ***fish cakes***, baked or grilled	110
6 oz (175 g) ***trout***, grilled	150
2 oz (50 g) shelled ***prawns***	55
4 oz (100 g) ***fish in batter***, for grilling or baking	195
100 g can ***tuna***, in brine	100
100 g can ***pink salmon***, in brine	150
120 g can ***sardines***, in tomato sauce	210
4 oz (100 g) ***fillet of mackerel*** or ***herring***, grilled	190
170 g can ***crab meat***	90
1 serving ***cod in parsley sauce***, (boil in the bag)	150
155 g can ***pilchards*** in tomato sauce	195

PART C

Eggs

	Calories
2 (size 3) ***eggs***	160

Pulses

	Calories
4 oz (100 g) ***baked beans*** in tomato sauce, sugar free	55
4 oz (100 g) ***red kidney, haricot*** or ***butter beans*** (cooked)	95
4 oz (100 g) ***cannellini beans***	90
4 oz (100 g) ***lentils***, (cooked)	100
4 oz (100 g) ***chickpeas***	105
½ oz (15 g) ***nuts*** or ***seeds***	85

Bread

Choose bread made with unrefined flour.

	Calories
1 large slice (35 g) ***wholemeal bread***, from a medium cut loaf	75
1 large slice (35 g) ***high fibre white bread***, from a medium cut loaf	75
1 mini ***wholemeal pitta bread***	90
1 large ***wholemeal pitta bread***	165
1 Hovis ***mini loaf***	115
1 ***Vitbe Hi-bran roll***	115
1 ***wholemeal roll***	125
1 toasted ***crumpet***	75
1 ***wholemeal muffin***	150
2 inch slice (40 g) ***wholemeal French bread***	100
1 slice ***malt loaf***	95

Pasta, rice and cereals

Choose unrefined types.

	Calories
1½ oz (40 g) dry weight ***wholewheat pasta***	140
1½ oz (40 g) dry weight ***egg noodles***	155
1½ oz (40 g) dry weight ***brown rice***	145
2 oz (50 g) dry weight ***bulgar wheat***	175
1 oz (25 g) ***oat cereal*** (uncooked weight)	100
1 oz (25 g) ***semolina, sago*** or ***tapioca*** (uncooked weight)	90

BREAKFAST CEREALS

Cereal type	**Calories per ounce (25 g)**
Crunchy cereals	120
Wholewheat cereals	80 – 95
Muesli	80 – 95
Bran flake cereals	80
Bran cereals	65

PART C

Dairy foods

Choose low fat dairy foods.	*Calories*
½ pint (300 ml) ***skimmed milk***	100
1 oz (25 g) ***low fat Cheddar***	75
1 oz (25 g) ***half fat edam***	65
1 oz (25 g) ***brie*** or ***camembert***	75
150 g pot ***natural low fat yogurt***	75
150 g pot ***low fat fruit yogurt***	130 – 150
125 g pot ***diet yogurt***	50
4 oz (100 g) ***very low fat fromage frais***	50
4 oz (100 g) ***cottage cheese***	100
4 oz (100 g) ***half fat cottage cheese***	85
2 oz (50 g) ***curd cheese***	100
1 oz (25 g) ***low fat cheese spread***	50

CHEESE

The calorie content of different cheeses varies depending on the fat content. Since some cheeses have more than twice as many calories as others it is worth getting to know which are the low calorie ones.

High fat cheeses	**Medium fat cheeses**	**Low fat cheeses**
100 to 130 Calories per ounce (25 g)	*55 to 100 Calories per ounce (25 g)*	*25 to 55 Calories per ounce (25 g)*
Cream cheese, boursin, blue brie, Cheddar, Stilton, Cotswold, double Gloucester, Leicester, lymeswold, red Windsor, sage Derby, gruyère, Wensleydale	Curd cheese, fetta, brie, camembert, edam, gouda, Mozzarella, half fat edam, half fat Cheddar, processed cheese, Roquefort, Danish blue, cheese spread	Quark, fromage frais, cottage cheese, ricotta, low fat cheese spread

PART C

YOGURT

A small pot of yogurt makes an excellent snack, a refreshing addition to a lunch box, or an easy dessert. The calorie content varies depending on which type you choose.

Fruit yogurt	Calories
150 g pot wholemilk yogurt	180 – 190
150 g pot thick, creamy yogurt (eg Gold Ski)	170 – 180
150 g pot low fat yogurt	130 – 150
125 g pot sugar free yogurt (eg St. Ivel Real)	100
125 g pot very low fat, sugar free yogurt (eg Diet Ski)	50

Natural yogurt	Calories
100 g strained Greek yogurt	135
150 g pot wholemilk yogurt	130
150 g pot low fat yogurt, stirred or set	80

CREAM

Cream should be reserved for special occasions. Choose a lower fat type or an alternative.

Type of Cream	Percentage fat	Calories per 2 teaspoons
Clotted	64	70
Double	48	35
Whipping	35	30
Half fat double	24	25
Sterilized, canned	23	25
Single	21	20
Sour	21	20
Half cream	13	15
Half fat single	9	10

Alternatives to cream	Percentage fat	Calories per 2 teaspoons
Greek strained yogurt	10	15
Creamed fromage frais	8	10
Natural yogurt	1	5
Very low fat fromage frais	0.5	5

Oils and fats

As they are very high in calories, oils and fats should only be used sparingly.

	Calories
1 Tbsp ***oil***	120
½ oz (15 g) ***butter*** or ***margarine***	110
1 oz (25 g) ***low fat spread***	100

CHIPS

Chips are best avoided at all times. But if you are a chip lover and like to indulge occasionally, there are various ways you can keep the calories down. If you make your own chips, make a few for yourself that are double size so that they soak up less fat. Oven chips are lower in fat and calories and are the most convenient to cook. Avoid crinkle cut and extra thin chips as, weight for weight, they contain more fat and more calories.

Type of chips	**Calories per ounce (25 g)**
Thin chips	80
Crinkle cut	80
Average chips	75
Oven chips	50
Double size chips	40

SALAD DRESSINGS

Save calories by choosing low calorie types such as low calorie salad cream, low calorie mayonnaise and oil free French dressing.

Type of dressing	Normal variety per tablespoon	Low calorie variety per tablespoon	Saving
Mayonnaise	120	45	75
Thousand island	60	25	35
Salad cream	50	25	25
Blue cheese dressing	70	20	50
Prawn cocktail sauce	50	20	30
Garlic dressing	65	10	55
French dressing	75	5	70

Vegetables

Eat plenty of vegetables, as ounce for ounce they are much lower in calories than many other foods.

Less than 20 Calories per 4 ounces (100 g)

Cauliflower, mushrooms, aubergines, French beans, asparagus, celery, marrow, Jerusalem artichokes, lettuce, tomatoes, cucumber, radishes, watercress, peppers, pickled onions, pickled red cabbage, pickled gherkins

20 to 30 Calories per 4 ounces (100 g)

Turnips, swedes, carrots, broccoli, Brussels sprouts, spinach, cabbage, leeks, courgettes, onions

50 Calories per 4 ounces (100 g)

Broad beans, peas, parsnips, beetroot, frozen mixed vegetables

75 Calories per 4 ounces (100 g)

Canned sweetcorn

	Calories
6 oz (175 g) potatoes, boiled or baked	150
7 oz (200 g) ratatouille, canned	90
8 oz (225 g) corn on the cob	150

Fruit

	Calories
1 average ***apple, pear, orange, peach,*** or ***nectarine***	50
4 oz (100 g) ***grapes***	65
1 ***fresh mango***	100
1 ***grapefruit***	35
1 ***satsuma*** or ***kiwi fruit***	30
4 oz (100 g) ***plums***	40
4 oz (100 g) ***strawberries*** or ***raspberries***	25
4 oz (100 g) peeled ***banana***	80
6 oz (175 g) stewed ***rhubarb*** with artificial sweetener	15
2 ***pineapple rings*** canned in natural juice	50
5 ***apricot halves*** canned in natural juice	35
2 ***peach halves*** canned in natural juice	40
4 oz (100 g) ***cherries***	40
8 oz (225 g) slice ***melon***	30
2 oz (50 g) ***raisins***	125
2 oz (50 g) ***dried prunes***	80
2 oz (50 g) ***dried apricots***	90

PART C

3 Healthy eating

What we eat plays a large part in keeping our bodies in good order and can affect how healthy we feel. Eating a well balanced, healthy diet can help reduce the risk of getting certain diseases and conditions such as heart disease, diabetes and bowel disorders.

Healthy eating is good for everyone – but what exactly does it mean?

A well balanced diet

The foods we eat can be divided into five main groups – proteins, dairy foods, carbohydrates, fruit and vegetables, and fats and oils. Some foods from each group should be eaten every day to ensure that the diet is well balanced and that it provides all the essential nutrients, including vitamins and minerals. ***As well as being good for your health, eating a well balanced diet can help in the battle to maintain your weight.*** (You may find it helpful to refer to the charts in the previous section.)

Protein foods

Meat, poultry, fish, eggs and offal provide good quality protein and an array of vitamins and minerals. Many other foods provide protein, but it is not of such good quality. Cereals and grains (***rice, wheat, bread, oats***), pulses (***beans, lentils*** and ***peas***), and nuts and seeds are all sources of incomplete proteins. When ***different sources of poorer quality protein*** are eaten together, they complement each other and the overall ***protein quality in the meal often becomes equivalent to the high quality protein of meat and fish***. An example of this is combining grains and pulses in a meal, like beans on toast.

By selecting protein foods carefully, you can cut back on calories, reduce fat and increase fibre intake. ***Choose lean cuts of meat and always trim off any visible fat. Skin poultry in order to reduce the fat content***. Vegetable protein foods are high in fibre.

Dairy foods

Dairy foods include milk and all the products made from it, such as yogurt, cream and cheese. Dairy foods are high in protein and are a source of good quality vitamins and minerals, especially calcium.

Choosing low fat dairy products, such as skimmed milk, low fat yogurt and cheeses, helps you to cut down on both fat and calories.

Carbohydrate foods

There are two types of carbohydrate.

Starchy or complex carbohydrates are found in bread, pasta, rice, pulses, oats and other cereals. Ounce for ounce carbohydrate provides the same calories as protein, and that is less than ***half the calories of fat***. Bread, potatoes, rice, pasta and breakfast cereals are also ***filling and satisfying***. Including them as part of a meal helps to discourage you from nibbling between meals.

Sugary types of carbohydrate can have natural or added sugars. Natural sugars are found in fruits and vegetables, whilst ***added sugars are in foods that we recognise as sweet such as desserts, cakes, biscuits, fruit yogurts, sweets, chocolates*** and so on. Foods high in sugar should be ***restricted***, as they tend to ***provide calories without other nutrients***. To keep the diet healthy restrict added sugars and eat more of the starchy types of carbohydrates.

Eating unrefined foods in place of refined foods helps to cut calories. Wholemeal bread, brown rice, wholewheat pasta, as well as wholegrain and bran enriched breakfast cereals all contain more dietary fibre than their refined counterparts, and so ounce for ounce they provide fewer calories. ***The extra bulk of these foods means you feel full after eating a smaller amount***, which also helps you to limit your calorie intake.

All types of bread are good for you. Wholemeal has the least calories and because of its high fibre content it takes a smaller amount to satisfy the appetite. Using sliced bread is a good trick for helping to control calorie intake since the slices are a uniform size and have a set number of calories. (One medium thick slice from a large wholemeal loaf weighs 35 g and provides 75 Calories.) Wholemeal rolls, wholemeal pitta bread and wholemeal French bread make a pleasant change from sliced bread. If you are used to eating white bread and find wholemeal too heavy, change to granary, malted grain or high fibre white bread, and try wholemeal again later.

Breakfast Cereals

Bran cereals, such as All-Bran, are lowest in calories and highest in fibre. Wholegrain cereals such as Wholewheat Flakes, Puffed Wheat, Shredded Wheat and Weetabix have the goodness of the whole grain, including the wheat bran which makes them a good source of fibre. Muesli contains wholegrain cereals with dried fruit and nuts and is also rich in fibre. Porridge oats are economical and when cooked with skimmed milk make a very nutritious low fat, high fibre breakfast.

The best types to choose are unsweetened or bran enriched. Crunchy cereals are higher in fat and calories and are not the best choice. Avoid highly refined and sugar coated cereals.

Fruit and vegetables

Fruit and vegetables are excellent foods for the calorie conscious. They are (with a few exceptions) relatively low in calories, provide fibre, and are rich in vitamins and minerals. Many yellow vegetables such as carrots, or dark green vegetables such as spinach and broccoli are rich in beta carotene which can be converted into Vitamin A. Including a variety of vegetables or a side salad as part of your meal makes it more interesting without adding many extra calories.

Oils and fats

Oils used in sauces, dressings and for cooking, and fats such as margarine and butter are the most obvious sources of fat. Fat is also found in some dairy foods, such as full fat milk, in meat and in nuts and seeds. Many prepared foods, such as cakes and biscuits are high in fat. ***Cutting down on your fat intake is good for your health, and is the most effective way to keep your calorie intake under control.***

There is a wide choice of alternatives to butter. To cut calorie intake ***low fat spread*** is the best choice. Most types have half the fat content of butter or margarine which cuts the calorie content by half. St Ivel Lowest has only one third of the fat of butter and provides 70 Calories per ounce (25 g).

Vitamins and minerals

Vitamins and minerals are not a separate food group, as they are found in a wide range of foods. They are only needed in very small amounts, but are vital for a variety of body functions.

To ensure that you get adequate levels of these essential substances, it is advisable to eat a variety of different foods chosen from the five food groups, otherwise you could risk missing out. For example, cutting out red meat and dairy products because they can be high in fat and calories is too drastic a step. Meat is the best source of iron in the diet, and dairy products are the best source of calcium. In order to reduce calorie intake it is better to choose lean cuts of meat and low fat dairy products. That way you are not missing out on the valuable vitamins, minerals and trace elements that these foods provide. ***On low calorie intakes you need to take particular care to ensure that your diet is supplying an adequate level of vitamins and minerals.*** The less food you eat, the less likely it is that you are getting enough. There are various ways you can counteract this.

Some foods are ***fortified*** with vitamins and minerals. These include many breakfast cereals, some low fat dairy products, and some fruit drinks. Look out for fortified products and choose them in preference to other types to help boost your intake.

Other ways to boost your vitamin and mineral intake are to take a ***multi vitamin and mineral preparation***, or to include ***one of the nutritious Cambridge products, such as a Cambridge Nutrition Bar, a sachet of Cambridge Diet Extra or a Cambridge Meal Bar.***

Salt is a mineral (sodium) which we need, but many people already consume more than enough. Excess salt in the diet can contribute to high blood pressure. High salt foods include ham, bacon and salami. Look out for added salt in tinned foods, fizzy drinks and salted peanuts. ***Try to avoid adding extra salt to your food.***

MINERALS

Mineral	What it does	Sources
Iron	• Important for the transport of oxygen around the body by the red blood cells	Liver, kidney, oily fish, dried fruits, nuts and seeds, dark green vegetables, lean red meats
Calcium	• Essential for strong bones • Helps in blood clotting • Keeps the cells healthy • Necessary for the nerves to function	Milk, yogurt, hard cheese, spinach, small fish (eg whitebait, canned sardines), pulses, muesli, almonds, brazil nuts, dried fruits, watercress
Zinc	• Helps the body to heal wounds and fight infections	Lean meat, liver, kidney, pulses, pilchards, sardines, oysters and other shellfish, cheese, nuts

Vitamin	What it does	Sources
A	• Keeps the skin healthy • Helps the body to fight infections • Important for good vision and healthy eyes	Butter, margarine, liver, whole milk, cheese, yogurt, carrots, spinach, broccoli, watercress, chinese leaves, mango, dried apricots
B1, B2, niacin	• Important for the release of energy in the body • Essential to maintain a healthy nervous system	*B1:* Bread, cereals, marmite, lean meats, offal, poultry *B2:* Milk, cheese, yogurt, eggs *Niacin:* seafoods, cereals, lean meats, liver, kidney
B6	• Enables the body to use protein • Important for the nervous system	Liver, kidney, wheatgerm, meat, fish, poultry, brown rice, vegetables, nuts
B12	• Essential for the formation of new cells, particularly blood cells and the health of nerve cells	Eggs, oily fish, liver, kidney, milk, cheese, meats, marmite, fermented and fortified foods
Folic acid	• Works with B12 to produce new cells	Spinach, Brussels sprouts, oranges, bran, liver, cabbage, endive, kidney, wheatgerm, almonds, peanuts, bran, breakfast cereals, asparagus
C	• Helps body to fight infections • Increases iron absorption • Helps in the repair of injuries and helps wounds to heal	Peppers, broccoli, melon, mango, strawberries, peas, oranges, lemons, blackcurrants, tomatoes, Brussels sprouts, fortified foods and drinks, cauliflower, spinach, watercress
D	• Essential for calcium absorption • Also made in the skin when exposed to sunlight	Butter, margarine, cheese, eggs, oily fish, cod liver oil, liver, some low fat spreads, whole milk, fortified foods
E	• Keeps tissues healthy • An antioxidant	Green leafy vegetables, cheese, sunflower oil, butter, almonds, peanuts, sunflower seeds, muesli, olives, wheatgerm
K	• Enables the blood to clot	Wholegrain cereals, soya beans, green leafy vegetables, liver, eggs, dairy foods

SUMMARY – HEALTHY EATING

Many of the changes that you need to make to keep your calorie intake in check are the same ones that everyone should be making for the sake of their health.

- *Eat a balanced diet*
- *Eat less fat*
- *Eat more complex carbohydrates and fibre*
- *Restrict your sugar intake*
- *Eat more fruit and vegetables*
- *Ensure you're getting enough vitamins and minerals*
- *Restrict your salt intake*

4 Planning and control

Eating planned, regular meals helps you to keep to the foods you should be eating as well as controlling the amount you eat. It also prevents you from getting ravenously hungry, and then picking or bingeing on high calorie snacks. Planning a nice meal, and then having it to look forward to, can be a great morale booster.

Eating regular meals

Breakfast – the most important meal of the day

Eating speeds up the metabolic rate. It helps you to feel more energetic, stops you flagging mid morning and increases your concentration. Having a bowl of cereal with skimmed milk, or wholemeal toast and low fat spread, prevents hunger pangs at coffee time and stops you reaching for less nutritious, calorie laden biscuits or chocolate.

Lunch – don't deprive yourself

Make it a nutritious meal such as a sandwich with wholemeal bread, and some fruit. Don't skip lunch to save calories. You will be hungry mid afternoon and be dipping into the biscuit tin, or picking at food before your evening meal.

Main meal – make it a good one

Base your main meal around a protein food such as lean meat, fish, eggs, low fat dairy foods or pulses. Serve it with potatoes, rice, pasta, noodles or bread and a selection of vegetables. If you eat a good meal, then you won't be tempted to tuck into the high calorie nibbles later in the evening.

Portion control

If you were a big eater before you started dieting, you must now learn to ***eat smaller portions***. To do this it's helpful to have an accurate idea of what 1 ounce of breakfast cereal looks like, how large a 6 ounce potato is, how many spoonfuls measure out 2 ounces of peas or sweetcorn. ***Use handy measures*** such as an empty yogurt pot, a jug or tablespoon to help you to be consistent. Try eating from a smaller plate, rather than a large plate which is only half full.

When cooking rice or pasta, weigh out and cook just the right amount. Allow 2 ounces (50 g) per person, dry weight, unless your recipe states otherwise. If you cook too much, you may be tempted to finish it up yourself.

Choose foods that come in ready portions. Having two Weetabix for breakfast is an easy way of controlling calorie intake, whereas there is nothing to stop you pouring a bigger bowl of loose cereal from the box. Other foods with a set number of calories include eggs, fish fingers, sausages and burgers (low fat types of course), pots of yogurt or cottage cheese, Shredded Wheat, bread rolls, sliced bread, and ready meals. Cooking the right number of chicken drumsticks, chicken portions, chops, turkey fillets or fish steaks helps to avoid the temptation of leftovers and second helpings.

Snacks

If nibbling caused your previous weight problem you must take positive action, otherwise your weight will soon be back to where you started. ***Constant nibbling of the wrong sorts of foods will add to your calorie intake,*** and you may not even notice what you eat.

TEMPTED TO NIBBLE

- Skimping too much to save calories at meals can do more harm than good if hunger pangs an hour or so later drive you straight for the kitchen, so plan filling meals.
- If you do get hungry between meals, have a 'legitimate' snack such as low fat cheese and a roll; dried or fresh fruit; raw vegetable sticks, tomatoes, celery and carrots; or a small sandwich. Arrange your snack attractively on a plate and sit down to eat it.
- If you really cannot stop yourself nibbling no matter how hard you try, then allow yourself 100 Calories for nibbles – say four nibbles of 25 Calories each.

Meal planning

Planning what meals you are going to eat during the coming week will help you to establish new sensible eating habits.

MEAL PLANNER

Monday	Tuesday	Wednesday	Thursday
Friday	Saturday	Sunday	

Shopping lists

Use your meal plan to write a shopping list. Add any basics which you use regularly. Writing a weekly shopping list will help ensure that you have plenty of low calorie foods and ingredients in store. Shopping to a list will also ***help prevent you from stocking up with calorie laden goodies*** that could be your downfall if you know they are sitting on the shelf in the cupboard. It's also a good way to keep your food spending under control.

The following list includes ***examples of the sorts of foods you should be buying*** to enable you to eat healthily and keep your calorie intake in check.

Meat

Turkey breast fillets, chicken breasts, chicken thighs, roasting chicken, liver, kidney, lean beef, lean pork fillet, low fat sausages.

Fish

Plaice fillets, cod steaks (fresh or frozen), tuna canned in brine.

Eggs

Pulses

Tinned red kidney beans, cannellini beans, baked beans in sugar free tomato sauce.

Bread

Large sliced wholemeal loaf, wholemeal rolls, Ryvita, wholemeal pittas, wholemeal muffins.

Pasta, rice and cereals

Wholewheat spaghetti and macaroni, brown rice.

Breakfast cereals: Weetabix, muesli, Puffed Wheat, Bran Flakes, porridge oats.

Dairy foods

Skimmed milk, diet yogurt, low fat natural yogurt, very low fat fromage frais, low fat Cheddar, curd cheese, parmesan, cottage cheese.

Oils and fats

Low fat spread.

Vegetables

Fresh vegetables: cabbage, carrots, mushrooms, green pepper, potatoes, turnips, broccoli, cauliflower.

Salad vegetables: tomatoes, cucumber, lettuce, radish, watercress, celery.

Frozen vegetables: whole green beans, spinach, sweetcorn, peas.

Canned vegetables: ratatouille, tinned tomatoes.

Fruit

Fresh fruit: bananas, apples, satsumas, mango, grapefruit, oranges, nectarines, peaches, grapes, pears.

Dried fruit: raisins, apricots, prunes.

Canned fruit: pineapple in natural juice, peach slices in natural juice.

Low calorie products

Low calorie soups, low calorie coleslaw, low calorie desserts (such as lemon or orange sorbet), pure fruit spread, artificial sweetener.

Sauces, dressings and seasoning

Chilli and garlic sauce, soy sauce, low calorie salad cream, oil free French dressing, low calorie mayonnaise, tomato purée, fresh and dried herbs.

Drinks

Mineral water, unsweetened orange juice, calorie free fizzy drinks.

SUMMARY

Regular meals help you control what you eat and will help prevent you from snacking.

- *Eat regular meals*
- *If you feel hungry have a healthy snack*
- *Plan your meals in advance*
- *Make a proper shopping list*

5 Cooking and family food

Family food

One of the major obstacles to staying slim can be working your food choices in with meals for the rest of the family. If you all tend to sit down together for a good family meal round the table, then it is all too easy to over indulge. Yet if you have something completely different, that too can be difficult. It is perfectly natural that you should want to enjoy the same meals as your family. Eating a skimpy salad while the family tuck into beef casserole, especially if you made the casserole yourself, is no fun. If your family is the type which doesn't have proper meals, and tends to eat different things at different times, it is tempting to keep nibbling throughout the evening yourself rather than eat a proper meal.

If family food threatens to come between you and your trim figure, there are various strategies you can adopt.

PART C

What is good for you in terms of calories, is likely to be good for your family's health too. If you are responsible for the cooking and shopping, then you are in the ideal position to make changes in the family diet and encourage everyone to eat healthier food.

To keep the calories of your own meal down, ***have less of the higher calorie parts of the meal*** such as meat, cheese, or sauce, and ***fill up with lower calorie vegetables, salad, potatoes or bread.*** And don't have seconds.

If you know the family evening meal is going to be high in calories, then ***eat less at breakfast and lunch*** so that you can still enjoy the meal with your family, or ***have a smaller portion of the main dish served with a large salad*** using your favourite vegetables.

If your family are pudding lovers, ***make sure there is always a low calorie alternative dessert available,*** such as fresh or stewed fruit or a low calorie yogurt.

Cooking techniques

The way food is cooked can make a big difference to the calorie content. ***Learning to cook in a low calorie way will help you to cut your calorie intake.*** Your family may not even notice the difference.

Don't fry – grill or bake burgers, sausages, bacon, chicken pieces, steaklets, fish fingers, fish steaks, fish in batter and meat chops.

Steaming is a good way to cook vegetables, fish and poultry. Add fresh herbs or a spicy sauce to give extra flavour.

Making casseroles and stews enables you to cut calories if you use lean cuts of meat and trim off any visible fat before cooking. Limit calories further by using only the minimum of oil to soften the vegetables and brown the meat. Make your casserole or stew the day before you plan to eat it, chill overnight and remove solidified fat from the surface. Serve yourself with less of the meat and more of the vegetables to help keep calories down.

Microwave cookers are ideal for cooking fish and vegetables without the need to add extra fat. A baked potato can be ready in minutes, making a quick and easy alternative for you if the family is having chips. A slice of bread or a bread roll can be thawed in seconds, giving you a filling substitute for another part of the meal which is higher in calories.

Barbecuing is nice for a change, but do not use this cooking technique too often. Choose lean cuts such as lean steaks, lean chops, low fat burgers and low fat sausages, and remove the skin from poultry. Beware of items that are smothered with barbecue sauce – you cannot see whether you are biting into fat or meat!

Stir frying is an exception to the no frying rule. Food is cooked in only a small amount of oil very quickly, so preserving the nutrients. Include plenty of vegetables to keep the fibre content up and the fat content down. Stir fry dishes flavoured with chilli sauce or Chinese five spice powder, are something different to look forward to. Serve with brown rice or noodles.

Pressure cooking makes a nourising meal which is ready quickly. Make double quantities of stews and casseroles and freeze half to make a quick and easy meal the following week.

Slow cookers are ideal for working mums, so there's a meal ready when you get home in the evening. They produce nourishing, hot meals which, if lean meats and the minimum of oil or fat are used, are also low in calories.

Cambridge Slim Cuisine

Cookery writer, Sue Kreitzman has developed a unique approach to weight maintenance. Cambridge Slim Cuisine virtually eliminates added fat. The food tastes really delicious and you can enjoy large portions without eating very many calories.

These are the main techniques that are used to keep calorie counts down.

Sautéeing in stock

Many everyday recipes begin with softening vegetables in oil or butter. But the Slim Cuisine method uses stock instead, cutting back on fat and calories. For the vegetables to taste truly sautéed rather than boiled and flabby, the stock is reduced, a splash of wine is added and the vegetables are tossed until there is a tasty aroma and they are browning on the bottom of the pan.

Alternatives to cream and mayonnaise

Draining natural yogurt or fromage frais through muslin produces a solid 'cream cheese' that is very low in fat, but which has a creamy texture. It can be thinned with buttermilk and vinegar to produce a low calorie mayonnaise style dressing.

Baked vegetables

Rather than slicing or sautéeing vegetables in oil, they can be oven baked, whole and in their skins just like jacket potatoes. They cook in their own juices and are tender and succulent. Puréed baked vegetables can be used to thicken sauces without adding fat calories.

Ice-cream

Rather than making ice-cream from full fat dairy products, Sue Kreitzman suggests puréeing frozen fruits, such as raspberries, with a little cold buttermilk and artificial sweetener, in a food processor. The resulting instant dessert is very low in fat, and tastes fruity and absolutely delicious. (This type of ice-cream should be eaten immediately, it should not be re-frozen.)

To find out more about Cambridge Slim Cuisine, ***ask your Counsellor or local bookshop for a copy of Sue Kreitzman's Cambridge Slim Cuisine, published by Transworld.***

Budget food

A complaint that's sometimes made about healthy or low calorie food is that it's expensive. Some low calorie foods are expensive, but most cheaper staple foods are ideal for weight maintenance. So ***don't let balancing the budget be an excuse for letting your trim figure slip.*** After all, eating less should cost you less!

Meat – the ***cheapest cuts tend to be fatty,*** so buy less of a leaner cut and ***stretch it with extra vegetables or pulses. Liver and kidneys*** are economical high protein foods that are low in calories. Make a steak and kidney pie with a potato rather than a pastry topping. Liver is just as tasty casseroled or braised as it is fried. ***Frozen rabbit meat*** is another good buy that is low in calories and ideal for stews and casseroles.

Poultry is good value for money. To keep fat and calories to a minimum ***don't eat the skin.*** Turkey steaks or breast fillets are solid lean meat, very low in fat, and economical. They can be cooked in a variety of different ways, such as marinated and then baked, casseroled, or stir fried.

Pulses, such as haricot and red kidney beans, lentils and dried peas and chickpeas are real cheapies, especially if you buy them dried and cook them yourself. They are ***rich in fibre, starchy carbohydrate, vitamins and minerals, provide protein and are low in fat.*** Use them with meat to make a cassoulet and chilli con carné, or to make vegetarian dishes such as vegetarian lasagne or bean rissoles. Cook with the minimum of oil and low fat dairy products to avoid adding too many extra calories.

Stretch ***fish*** by serving it with a low fat cheese sauce, or bake it with plenty of vegetables. ***Coley is a particularly cheap fish*** which is ideal for fish pies or fish cakes. ***For a special meal,***

trout is quite economical and not high in calories. Mackerel and herring are excellent value for money, but oily fish like these are higher in calories than white fish, so serve a smaller portion.

Serving bread, pasta, rice or potatoes with a main course is an economical way of ensuring everyone has a satisfying meal and of keeping the calories in check.

Save money by ***buying fruit and vegetables in season*** when they are cheapest. Buy ***potatoes by the sack,*** and ***buy large packets of frozen peas and beans.***

Save money by ***weaning your family off snacks such as biscuits,*** cakes, crisps and chocolate bars. Providing a good nourishing meal that will keep them going right through to the next meal makes economic sense, as well as being better nutritionally.

Healthy and economical family meals

The following suggestions show how to keep the calories down and make the meals healthier for your family at the same time.

Beef burgers Grill low fat burgers and serve in a wholemeal bun with a salad rather than with chips.

Chicken casserole Remove fat from the chicken, and skin it before cooking, include plenty of vegetables, softening them in a minimum of oil or stock.

Chilli con carné Use lean mince, dry fry and drain off the fat, use less mince and add extra red kidney beans, serve with brown rice.

Curry and rice Trim left over meat of visible fat, use the minimum of oil to soften the vegetables and serve with brown rice.

Fish and chips Grill or steam the fish (rather than frying it) and serve with a few oven chips or a wholemeal roll and a salad.

Fish in cheese sauce Cook the fish in skimmed milk, thicken cooking liquid with a roux and stir in low fat Cheddar and grated parmesan for a good flavour.

Lamb stew Trim any fat from the lamb, add plenty of root vegetables, and (if desired) canned tomatoes. Adding lentils or marrowfat peas and using less meat keeps the fat content down and avoids the need to thicken with flour.

Liver and bacon Brush liver with a little oil and grill (rather than fry), or make a casserole. Serve fresh steamed or boiled vegetables and mushrooms cooked in stock.

Roasts With all the trimmings they are associated with 'blow out' Sunday lunches, but by eating moderately you can keep calories down. Chicken and turkey are particularly low in calories. There is no need to add any fat to the pan when you are cooking the meat. Eat only the lean meat. Skim fat from the meat juices to make the gravy and don't make it too thick. Eat potatoes boiled or baked rather than roast. Cook a selection of vegetables. Don't have seconds!

Salads Choose a low fat protein food such as boiled eggs, lean ham, roast chicken, or tuna fish canned in brine. Make potato salad and coleslaw with low calorie mayonnaise and low fat natural yogurt. Serve with a wide selection of salad vegetables, and wholemeal bread or a baked potato.

Sausage and mash Grill low fat sausages, mash potatoes with skimmed milk and low fat spread (rather than top of the milk and butter).

Shepherd's pie Trim fat from cooked meat, mash potatoes with skimmed milk and low fat spread. Top with cheese and wholemeal breadcrumbs.

Spaghetti Bolognese Use lean mince, dry fry and drain off the fat. Add a grated carrot and sliced celery stalk for extra flavour and nutrients. Adding lentils and using less mince increases the fibre content. Serve with wholemeal pasta.

Convenience foods

Although convenience foods have been with us for decades, many people mistakenly believe that these have no part in a healthy diet. Processed foods are thought to be inferior to fresh. But it is unnecessary to limit yourself to purely fresh foods.

Canning, drying and freezing are simply ways of preserving foods for your convenience. Canning destroys the bacteria and enzymes in food which cause deterioration. Dried foods are unable to support bacterial growth. Freezing simply 'suspends foods in time'. At freezing temperatures bacteria are unable to grow and the activity of enzymes is arrested, so that the food is prevented from deteriorating.

But are convenience foods nutritious? It is actually quite hard to lose most nutrients from food, apart from a few sensitive vitamins such as vitamin C and some of the group B vitamins. Developments in technology mean that preservation methods used today are less harsh than formerly. They have less effect on the food and fewer vitamins are lost. Research studies have compared the nutrient levels in fresh, canned and frozen vegetables after cooking. ***On the whole, provided the frozen and canned vegetables are not overcooked, the vitamin levels are just about equivalent.*** Preserved vegetables stay in the same condition as when they were processed, whereas fresh ones lose vitamin C from the time they are picked until they are cooked.

Convenience foods have many advantages. They are ***great time savers*** and are good when the family are all eating at different times. Some types have the calorie conscious in mind and are low in fat and calories. They are usually ***packaged in convenient amounts*** and so there is ***far less waste.*** They are also an aid to portion control and usually the ***calorie content is given on the packet.***

Cambridge Slim Meals

Cambridge Slim Meals are ideal for weight maintenance. Individually packaged to provide one 400 Calorie meal when mixed with water, and cooked and served with rice, potato or pasta as directed. They can be used for a solo lunch or supper. Slim Meals are a good example of how using packet meals can help with portion control. They make a great stand by for the larder, and making more portions can give you a cheap and easy family supper. There is a choice of dishes, including a vegetarian option. Cambridge Slim Meals are available exclusively from Cambridge Counsellors.

SUMMARY

- *Healthy eating guidelines are good for all the family*
- *Use cooking techniques that minimise added fat*
- *Low cost ingredients can be used to produce tasty and nourishing meals*
- *Convenience foods can save you time and help with calorie and portion control*

6 Mind and body

Your whole life is stretching ahead of you. Unlike your diet, which had a definite goal, you have to try to sustain your success with no short term deadline in sight. ***A really positive mental attitude and making the commitment to change certain aspects of your lifestyle will really help.*** There are a number of things you can do to enhance your chances of success.

Mental attitude

There are many things other than simple hunger that prompt us to eat. These include eating for comfort, out of boredom, just to be sociable, out of habit, and in response to moods such as anger, joy, frustration or depression. ***To stay slim you need to overcome these emotional urges to eat.*** It helps to realise that what you eat and drink are not the most important things in life. When you go out for a meal, take more pleasure over deciding what to wear, enjoy doing your make-up and hair and really appreciate looking and feeling good. Being with friends, sharing their company and enjoying the conversation can be more interesting than the food.

More interests

Look back at your life. Think about what led you into the kitchen in search of secret snacks or nibbles, and why you felt you needed to over eat. Think what you can add to your life that will compensate for these feelings. Losing weight has undoubtedly boosted your confidence and given you more enthusiasm for life. Put these feelings to good use by adding more interests to your life. Positive steps you can take include taking up new activities, or learning something new.

Weekly weigh in

Make it a golden rule to ***weigh and measure yourself once a week,*** at the same time of day, wearing more or less the same clothes. There's no point in weighing yourself more often.

Your image

Your appearance is an expression of your personality and how you feel about yourself. Taking care to present yourself well can do wonders for your confidence. Now that you have an attractive slim figure it is an ideal time to rethink your image.

Plan your new look and build it up gradually, giving thought to colour, styles and accessories. Choose clothes carefully – make sure they flatter your new figure. The styles can be trendy or classic, depending on what you need them for, but make sure that they make you look and feel good.

Advice from a ***colour analyst*** can give you ***new ideas*** and help you pick the colours which make you look your best. There is no need to look drab and dowdy, so go for colours that will attract attention and keep you feeling cheerful.

How long is it since you had your hair restyled? A different ***haircut*** can make the world of difference to how you look and feel. If you have lost weight from your face a new hair style will help to flatter your features.

PART C

What about ***make-up***? If your face is no longer chubby then you'll need to learn new ways to enhance its new shape. Why not have ***a make-up lesson***, or visit a make-up consultant in a store and ask for advice on what is best for you.

Men too can update their image. Get your partner or a woman friend to help you choose new items of clothing.

New flattering clothes, a good few sizes smaller, will give you more incentive to maintain your weight. Don't begrudge time and money spent on yourself. ***After all your efforts to diet you deserve to enjoy the rewards and really make the most of yourself.***

Treats

From a very early age we associate food with reward, especially foods such as chocolates and sweets. As adults we continue to use foods for treats or to cheer ourselves up. Unfortunately treat foods are usually high in calories. They may have been part of the cause of the original weight problem, and they can certainly come between you and maintaining your weight if you're not careful.

For many people food is the only way they know to reward themselves. But there are lots of other ***interesting and enjoyable ways to indulge yourself that don't involve consuming calories.*** Think about some of the following next time you are tempted to turn to food for a treat or just for something to do.

Instead of buying chocolates on impulse, buy something different, such as earrings, some new make-up, a scarf, perfume, a wonderful smelling soap, a luxurious bubble bath, a pair of stockings or some coloured tights, or pretty underwear. Men too should choose non-food items, such as sports equipment or magazines. When you are standing around waiting for a bus or train, or are on a journey it is very tempting to buy some sweets just to while away the time: ***don't***, buy a magazine or puzzle book instead.

Snacking is a great time waster. Use your time positively and effectively.

Exercise

One of your aims in losing weight was probably to improve your figure, so it's a real waste to ignore the ***positive contribution that regular exercise can make.*** To conquer the battle of the bulge for good you need a positive attitude to physical activity. This is the time to get up and get moving.

Many people view exercise as boring and too much effort. They believe its not worth the exertion of a 30 minute swim when all the expended calories are replaced in the 2 minutes it takes to devour a chocolate bar! But the truth is, the more active you are, the less carefully you may need to watch what you eat.

Regular is best

Exercise doesn't have to be strenuous or exhausting. Occasional bursts of activity do little good however much effort you put in. ***Choose some form of activity that you enjoy.*** If it is fun rather than a chore you will have more incentive to keep it up.

Try to make time to go for a ***30 minute walk every day.*** You should also do ***a more energetic form of activity at least twice a***

week, such as swimming, badminton or tennis, running, or going to an exercise or dance class. If you haven't exercised for some time, consult your doctor for a check-up first. Start off gently, increasing your level of activity gradually.

Keep active

Be as active as you can throughout the day, taking every opportunity you have to keep on the move. For example walk to the shops rather than going in the car, take the dog for a walk rather than just putting him out, walk up the stairs rather than taking the lift, get off the bus a couple of stops earlier and walk the rest of the way. Instead of lolling in the chair on Sunday afternoons in front of the television, do something active such as going for a walk or mowing the lawn.

THE BENEFITS OF REGULAR EXERCISE

- Improves your shape by toning and tightening muscles
- Keeps you occupied when you might otherwise be eating
- Helps to increase your daily calorie expenditure by increasing the proportion of lean tissue in the body
- Gives you a feeling of well being
- Keeps you in tune with your body
- Enables you to cope better with the strains and stresses of life
- Gives you an opportunity to meet new friends
- Helps you wind down and relax
- Helps you to sleep better at night

SUMMARY

- ***Be more positive about yourself***
- ***Develop new interests***
- ***Weigh and measure yourself weekly***
- ***Revise your image***
- ***Give yourself non-food treats***
- ***Take regular exercise***

7 Social eating and drinking

Eating out

Eating out is one of life's pleasures. It may be something you do regularly or once in a while on a special occasion. Either way you want to enjoy it to the full without feeling guilty, or worrying that it will add pounds to your weight. The trick is to ***be cautious, but allow yourself one real indulgence.***

Strategies for Eating Out

- Keep to healthy eating guidelines to limit the damage by making low fat choices such as fish, poultry, lean red meat, avoiding anything fried or anything in a creamy sauce
- ***Keep a check on how much you are drinking:*** pre-dinner alcoholic drinks stimulate the appetite as well as adding calories
- Have a ***glass of water with the meal to quench your thirst*** – as well as a glass of wine – that way you'll drink less wine
- ***Enjoy your indulgence***
- Don't feel that to get your money's worth you have to eat everything that is served to you, ***eat until you just feel full*** then put your knife and fork down and get the waiter to take your plate away before you change your mind!
- Compensate for your meal out by ***eating less during the day,*** and less the following day

RESTAURANT MEALS: GOOD CHOICES

Starters

Chilled melon

Grapefruit cocktail

Consommé

Soup that is not creamy

Asparagus – ask for the sauce or butter to be served separately

Corn on the cob – ask for no butter

Mussels

Ratatouille

Shell fish platter

Main courses

Chicken and fish dishes that are not fried or in a creamy sauce

Omelette

Grilled steak

Grilled or baked trout

Lobster

Kebabs

Roast meals

Calves' liver

Salads – but avoid ones in mayonnaise

Desserts – all without cream!

Fresh fruit

Fruit salad

Ice-cream

Sorbet

Figs

Caramel oranges

Poached pears

Strawberries

Summer pudding

Crème caramel

Entertaining

Meals that are shared with family and friends, such as dinner parties, Sunday lunches, Sunday teas, or even just having people around for a drink can be quite a problem for calorie watchers. On such occasions it is usual to prepare something a little special that is really tempting. Over eating at such events is a common problem.

Whether you are doing the entertaining, or are being entertained, there are various ways you can help to prevent taking in an excessive number of calories. Firstly don't over indulge. Ask for small portions, especially of the dessert, and eat slowly. Eat just enough to satisfy your appetite and always refuse seconds. Keep your drink calories down by sipping slowly, and refusing a refill now and then.

If you are the host it's easier to restrict your calorie intake. Take care to cook or choose lower calorie dishes that are still very tempting, and that are cooked in a low calorie way. Make a choice of desserts available including one that is low in calories such as a fresh fruit salad or a sorbet.

Fast foods and take aways

When you don't feel like cooking it makes a change to go out for something to eat. Fast food restaurants are a popular choice as they are economical and the atmosphere is relaxed. If you like to go out to eat regularly, can you still accommodate this into your eating routine without putting on weight?

The answer is that of course you can. Take a look at the other people eating out the next time you are in a pizza or a burger bar. Many of them will be slim. There is no reason why eating these types of foods should cause you to put on weight.

Obviously it helps to keep the calorie level of your meal down as much as possible, and ensure that you don't eat to excess. But at the same time you want to enjoy yourself and not feel too restrained. This can be done provided you compensate at other meals. You must expect to eat less during the day, or the following day, or both!

Alcohol

Limiting your alcohol intake helps to limit calorie intake as well as being better for your health. The amount of alcohol the body can tolerate regularly is a lot less than many people think. Drinking too much on a regular basis over a period of time can cause lasting damage; it increases the risk of harm to virtually every body function.

Drinking is associated with having a good time. It is easy to get carried along with everyone else and have more drinks than is good for you, or good for your figure. Depending on what is your favourite tipple, ***four rounds of drinks in the pub can easily tot up to 400 Calories plus.*** And that is before you tuck into the crisps or nuts!

Don't feel you always have to have an alcoholic drink, ***consider sticking to calorie free drinks,*** such as a Perrier or a diet mixer. Alcohol free beers and wines are ideal for the calorie conscious as they have about half the calories of normal beers and wines. On special occasions allow yourself an alcoholic drink or two at the most.

If you are having drinks at home or at a friend's or relative's house, remember that ***home poured measures tend to be on the generous side,*** which means more calories than pub measures. Buy a spirit measure so that you can gauge the amount you are pouring. ***Alcohol stimulates the appetite*** so it is best to keep to non-alcoholic aperitifs.

The Royal College of Physicians recommends that ***men should not drink more than 21 units of alcohol a week,*** and ***women not more than 14.*** It is best to have three or four days a week without drinking any alcohol at all. The alcoholic content of drinks is measured in units. 1 unit is 1 pub measure (1 fl oz 25 ml) of spirit, sherry, martini, ½ pint lager or beer or a 4 fl oz (100 ml) glass of a light wine. A glass of most wines counts as 1½ units. This means the maximum safe intake is 2½ pints of beer four days a week for men, and 2 martinis and 1 glass of wine four days a week for women. But remember that alcohol contains 7 calories per gram and ***the calorie conscious should set their own limits somewhat lower than this.***

Holidays

Holidays are a real testing time for the weight conscious. The holiday atmosphere and break in the usual routine makes it more difficult to keep calorie intake in check.

Self catering

If you have chosen a self catering holiday it is easier to watch what you eat. You are not at the mercy of hotel breakfasts and evening meals. You can please yourself what you have. If you have some meals out, follow the guidelines for eating out. If you are over indulgent you can always have a light meal the next day.

Breakfasts and evening meals

If you are staying in a hotel or bed and breakfast you will have to be more strict with yourself. ***You don't have to tuck into a cooked breakfast just because it is offered.*** Keep calories down by having cereal or fruit and toast. If you fancy something cooked, have it instead of the cereals and toast, not as an extra! For your evening meal, whether you are eating in the hotel or in a restaurant, follow the guidelines for eating out. If you eat a good breakfast and find the evening meals are also substantial try and make do without lunch, or keep it very small.

Treats

Indulging in too many ice-creams, sweets, cream teas, drinks and other calorie laden treats is another reason for you to come back pounds heavier. Try to keep your intake of these foods down to a minimum. Allow yourself ***one small food treat*** every other day.

Fun

Getting ***plenty of exercise*** on holiday will do you the world of good, as well as keeping you occupied and ***keeping your mind off food***. Keep as active as you can. Go for lots of walks and really explore your surroundings. If there's a pool, use it every day, and make the most of any other sports facilities that are available. You will come back from your holiday more relaxed and refreshed, and may have prevented some of those extra calories turning to fat!

Back home

When you ***step on the scales after your holiday is over, if you have put on 4 pounds or more, then take action immediately.*** Don't make any excuses. Turn to PART D for advice.

Christmas

Christmas is the time of year when almost everyone worries about their figure, so you are not alone. Since no one wants to spend the cold days of January on a diet it is worth exercising a little caution over these highly indulgent days. The secret is to have a little of what you fancy, but not too much of anything.

Planning

Begin with being cautious with the shopping. Take care not to buy too many Christmas treats, such as boxes of biscuits, tins of sweets, nuts, chocolates and cakes. If they are going to be left over, will you be able to refuse them? Don't look for excuses to buy them. Remember your visitors are also likely to be watching what they eat. Buy in plenty of the healthier Christmas foods such as satsumas and other fresh fruits, celery and pickles, and dried fruits. Alcohol free wines and beers will be welcomed by your driving guests, as well as being lower in calories for you.

Christmas lunch

This is the big meal of the year, when everyone eats a lot. But you can still be sensible without spoiling your fun. Have a light breakfast, eat a good lunch, and if you are hungry in the evening have a light supper. Steer clear of the chocolates and sweets.

CALORIE COUNTED CHRISTMAS LUNCH

1 ***glass dry sherry,*** 2 glasses ***dry white wine***

4 oz (100 g) ***turkey,*** 1 small ***roast potato,*** 4 oz (100 g) ***Brussels sprouts,*** 4 oz (100 g) ***carrots,*** 2 oz (50 g) ***peas,*** 2 Tbsp ***stuffing,*** 2 Tbsp ***thin gravy,*** 2 tsp ***cranberry sauce,*** ½ ***low fat sausage,*** ½ rasher ***streaky bacon***

4 oz (100 g) ***Christmas pudding*** with ¼ pint (150 ml) ***brandy sauce*** made with skimmed milk

The damage? Approximately 1200 Calories

Boxing Day

With all that cold turkey and lots of salads and pickles, you should be able to keep the calories in your meals quite low. That will allow you to have a mince pie and a slice of Christmas cake while still keeping your overall intake to a reasonable level.

The next day . . .

This is the time to get back to your usual eating routine. Continuing to over eat now will really pile on the pounds so be strict with yourself.

SUMMARY

- ***Choose wisely from the menu when eating out***
- ***Have one indulgence***
- ***Adjust your intake following a large meal***
- ***Keep alcohol for special occasions***
- ***Choose carefully when on holiday***
- ***Enjoy yourself too!***
- ***Involve yourself in non-food activities***
- ***Take action as soon as you get home from holiday if you've put on 4 pounds or more***
- ***Enjoy Christmas (in moderation)***
- ***Take steps to repair any damage***

KEEPING TRACK:
Your personal weight record

The structured eating programme – your record

Keeping track after that

And if you do gain weight . . .

PART D

The structured eating programme – your record

Use the personal charts in this part of the booklet to monitor your progress on the structured eating programme (PART B).

At the beginning of each week, fill out the details at the top of the chart.

STRUCTURED EATING PROGRAMME – PERSONAL CHART

WEEK NUMBER	
WEEK COMMENCING	
CALORIE LEVEL	

WEIGHT – Start of Week	

Each day record the calorie level you choose from for each meal. At the end of the day, total up your intake to check you've had the right amount.

MONDAY	Calories
milk allowance	
breakfast	
lunch	
main meal	
starter or dessert	
flexi calories	
TOTAL	

Obviously, it's in your best interests to stick to the programme. If by any chance you do 'cheat', then don't get disheartened and give up. Include the extra calorie intake in the flexi calorie section and in your daily total. Don't be too hard on yourself. We're all human – and sticking to the programme requires real commitment – resolve not to do it again.

Make a note of any exercise you take during the week.

Exercise

At the end of the week, record your final weight, and note any changes.

WEIGHT – End of Week	
CHANGE/NO CHANGE	

Also take your measurements and record them.

Women shold note if the week includes their period or the few days before it, as this can affect your weight.

Keeping track after that

Once you've finished the structured eating programme, use the weight maintenance charts to record your weight and measurements each week. Fill in the figures and then plot your weight on the graph.

That way, you can see any change, even if it's only gradual. Also, as the weeks go by, you'll get a real sense of achievement.

And if you do gain weight . . .

If you gain 4 pounds or more, aim to do something about it straight away. (The only exception to this is for women, if the weight gain occurs just before a period is due.) Certainly don't allow yourself to gain 6 or 7 pounds before taking action.

Either Go back onto the structured eating programme, starting at the 1000 Calorie base level, until you get just below your ideal weight. Then go onto the calorie level that enables you to maintain your weight, using the food choices from the structured eating programme. Once your weight has remained stable at your ideal weight for at least a week, you can then start to follow the advice given in PART C.

Or Use Cambridge Diet products to replace one or more of your meals each day, cutting down your calorie intake so that you lose the weight. For example, you could have a sachet of Cambridge Diet for breakfast, a Cambridge Meal Bar for lunch, and a Cambridge Diet soup plus a 400 Calorie evening meal. This would give you an intake of just over 800 Calories.

Or Go back onto the Cambridge Diet sole source programme, until your weight is 4 to 6 pounds below your target weight.

And Try to be positive and keep active. You may like to re-read PART C again for more help on calorie cutting tips to keep you at your ideal weight.

CAMBRIDGE WEIGHT MAINTENANCE CHART

Pounds								
+7								
+6								
+5								
+4								
+3								
+2								
+1								
Ideal weight								
−1								
−2								
−3								
−4								
−5								
−6								
−7								
WEIGHT								
Bust/chest								
Waist								
Hips								
Upper arms								
Thighs								
Period?								
WEEK								

WEEK NUMBER	
WEEK COMMENCING	
CALORIE LEVEL	

WEIGHT – Start of Week	
WEIGHT – End of Week	
CHANGE/NO CHANGE	

MONDAY	Calories
milk allowance	
breakfast	
lunch	
main meal	
starter or dessert	
flexi calories	
TOTAL	

TUESDAY	Calories
milk allowance	
breakfast	
lunch	
main meal	
starter or dessert	
flexi calories	
TOTAL	

WEDNESDAY	Calories
milk allowance	
breakfast	
lunch	
main meal	
starter or dessert	
flexi calories	
TOTAL	

THURSDAY	Calories
milk allowance	
breakfast	
lunch	
main meal	
starter or dessert	
flexi calories	
TOTAL	

FRIDAY	Calories
milk allowance	
breakfast	
lunch	
main meal	
starter or dessert	
flexi calories	
TOTAL	

SATURDAY	Calories
milk allowance	
breakfast	
lunch	
main meal	
starter or dessert	
flexi calories	
TOTAL	

SUNDAY	Calories
milk allowance	
breakfast	
lunch	
main meal	
starter or dessert	
flexi calories	
TOTAL	

Measurements	
bust/chest	
waist	
hips	
upper arm	
thighs	
Women – Period	
YES/NO	

Exercise

PART D

WEEK NUMBER	
WEEK COMMENCING	
CALORIE LEVEL	

WEIGHT – Start of Week	
WEIGHT – End of Week	
CHANGE/NO CHANGE	

MONDAY	Calories
milk allowance	
breakfast	
lunch	
main meal	
starter or dessert	
flexi calories	
TOTAL	

TUESDAY	Calories
milk allowance	
breakfast	
lunch	
main meal	
starter or dessert	
flexi calories	
TOTAL	

WEDNESDAY	Calories
milk allowance	
breakfast	
lunch	
main meal	
starter or dessert	
flexi calories	
TOTAL	

THURSDAY	Calories
milk allowance	
breakfast	
lunch	
main meal	
starter or dessert	
flexi calories	
TOTAL	

FRIDAY	Calories
milk allowance	
breakfast	
lunch	
main meal	
starter or dessert	
flexi calories	
TOTAL	

SATURDAY	Calories
milk allowance	
breakfast	
lunch	
main meal	
starter or dessert	
flexi calories	
TOTAL	

SUNDAY	Calories
milk allowance	
breakfast	
lunch	
main meal	
starter or dessert	
flexi calories	
TOTAL	

Measurements	
bust/chest	
waist	
hips	
upper arm	
thighs	
Women – Period	
YES/NO	

Exercise

WEEK NUMBER	
WEEK COMMENCING	
CALORIE LEVEL	

WEIGHT – Start of Week	
WEIGHT – End of Week	
CHANGE/NO CHANGE	

MONDAY	Calories
milk allowance	
breakfast	
lunch	
main meal	
starter or dessert	
flexi calories	
TOTAL	

TUESDAY	Calories
milk allowance	
breakfast	
lunch	
main meal	
starter or dessert	
flexi calories	
TOTAL	

WEDNESDAY	Calories
milk allowance	
breakfast	
lunch	
main meal	
starter or dessert	
flexi calories	
TOTAL	

THURSDAY	Calories
milk allowance	
breakfast	
lunch	
main meal	
starter or dessert	
flexi calories	
TOTAL	

FRIDAY	Calories
milk allowance	
breakfast	
lunch	
main meal	
starter or dessert	
flexi calories	
TOTAL	

SATURDAY	Calories
milk allowance	
breakfast	
lunch	
main meal	
starter or dessert	
flexi calories	
TOTAL	

SUNDAY	Calories
milk allowance	
breakfast	
lunch	
main meal	
starter or dessert	
flexi calories	
TOTAL	

Measurements	
bust/chest	
waist	
hips	
upper arm	
thighs	
Women – Period	
YES/NO	

Exercise

WEEK NUMBER	
WEEK COMMENCING	
CALORIE LEVEL	

WEIGHT – Start of Week	
WEIGHT – End of Week	
CHANGE/NO CHANGE	

MONDAY	Calories
milk allowance	
breakfast	
lunch	
main meal	
starter or dessert	
flexi calories	
TOTAL	

TUESDAY	Calories
milk allowance	
breakfast	
lunch	
main meal	
starter or dessert	
flexi calories	
TOTAL	

WEDNESDAY	Calories
milk allowance	
breakfast	
lunch	
main meal	
starter or dessert	
flexi calories	
TOTAL	

THURSDAY	Calories
milk allowance	
breakfast	
lunch	
main meal	
starter or dessert	
flexi calories	
TOTAL	

FRIDAY	Calories
milk allowance	
breakfast	
lunch	
main meal	
starter or dessert	
flexi calories	
TOTAL	

SATURDAY	Calories
milk allowance	
breakfast	
lunch	
main meal	
starter or dessert	
flexi calories	
TOTAL	

SUNDAY	Calories
milk allowance	
breakfast	
lunch	
main meal	
starter or dessert	
flexi calories	
TOTAL	

Measurements	
bust/chest	
waist	
hips	
upper arm	
thighs	
Women – Period	
YES/NO	

Exercise

WEEK NUMBER	
WEEK COMMENCING	
CALORIE LEVEL	

WEIGHT – Start of Week	
WEIGHT – End of Week	
CHANGE/NO CHANGE	

MONDAY	Calories
milk allowance	
breakfast	
lunch	
main meal	
starter or dessert	
flexi calories	
TOTAL	

TUESDAY	Calories
milk allowance	
breakfast	
lunch	
main meal	
starter or dessert	
flexi calories	
TOTAL	

WEDNESDAY	Calories
milk allowance	
breakfast	
lunch	
main meal	
starter or dessert	
flexi calories	
TOTAL	

THURSDAY	Calories
milk allowance	
breakfast	
lunch	
main meal	
starter or dessert	
flexi calories	
TOTAL	

FRIDAY	Calories
milk allowance	
breakfast	
lunch	
main meal	
starter or dessert	
flexi calories	
TOTAL	

SATURDAY	Calories
milk allowance	
breakfast	
lunch	
main meal	
starter or dessert	
flexi calories	
TOTAL	

SUNDAY	Calories
milk allowance	
breakfast	
lunch	
main meal	
starter or dessert	
flexi calories	
TOTAL	

Measurements	
bust/chest	
waist	
hips	
upper arm	
thighs	
Women – Period	
YES/NO	

Exercise

WEEK NUMBER	
WEEK COMMENCING	
CALORIE LEVEL	

WEIGHT – Start of Week	
WEIGHT – End of Week	
CHANGE/NO CHANGE	

MONDAY	Calories
milk allowance	
breakfast	
lunch	
main meal	
starter or dessert	
flexi calories	
TOTAL	

TUESDAY	Calories
milk allowance	
breakfast	
lunch	
main meal	
starter or dessert	
flexi calories	
TOTAL	

WEDNESDAY	Calories
milk allowance	
breakfast	
lunch	
main meal	
starter or dessert	
flexi calories	
TOTAL	

THURSDAY	Calories
milk allowance	
breakfast	
lunch	
main meal	
starter or dessert	
flexi calories	
TOTAL	

FRIDAY	Calories
milk allowance	
breakfast	
lunch	
main meal	
starter or dessert	
flexi calories	
TOTAL	

SATURDAY	Calories
milk allowance	
breakfast	
lunch	
main meal	
starter or dessert	
flexi calories	
TOTAL	

SUNDAY	Calories
milk allowance	
breakfast	
lunch	
main meal	
starter or dessert	
flexi calories	
TOTAL	

Measurements	
bust/chest	
waist	
hips	
upper arm	
thighs	
Women – Period	
YES/NO	

Exercise

WEEK NUMBER	
WEEK COMMENCING	
CALORIE LEVEL	

WEIGHT – Start of Week	
WEIGHT – End of Week	
CHANGE/NO CHANGE	

MONDAY	Calories
milk allowance	
breakfast	
lunch	
main meal	
starter or dessert	
flexi calories	
TOTAL	

TUESDAY	Calories
milk allowance	
breakfast	
lunch	
main meal	
starter or dessert	
flexi calories	
TOTAL	

WEDNESDAY	Calories
milk allowance	
breakfast	
lunch	
main meal	
starter or dessert	
flexi calories	
TOTAL	

THURSDAY	Calories
milk allowance	
breakfast	
lunch	
main meal	
starter or dessert	
flexi calories	
TOTAL	

FRIDAY	Calories
milk allowance	
breakfast	
lunch	
main meal	
starter or dessert	
flexi calories	
TOTAL	

SATURDAY	Calories
milk allowance	
breakfast	
lunch	
main meal	
starter or dessert	
flexi calories	
TOTAL	

SUNDAY	Calories
milk allowance	
breakfast	
lunch	
main meal	
starter or dessert	
flexi calories	
TOTAL	

Measurements	
bust/chest	
waist	
hips	
upper arm	
thighs	
Women – Period	
YES/NO	

Exercise

CAMBRIDGE WEIGHT MAINTENANCE CHART

Pounds								
+7								
+6								
+5								
+4								
+3								
+2								
+1								
Ideal weight								
−1								
−2								
−3								
−4								
−5								
−6								
−7								
WEIGHT								
Bust/chest								
Waist								
Hips								
Upper arms								
Thighs								
Period?								
WEEK								

CAMBRIDGE WEIGHT MAINTENANCE CHART

Pounds								
+7								
+6								
+5								
+4								
+3								
+2								
+1								
Ideal weight								
−1								
−2								
−3								
−4								
−5								
−6								
−7								
WEIGHT								
Bust/chest								
Waist								
Hips								
Upper arms								
Thighs								
Period?								
WEEK								

Cambridge Weight Maintenance Chart

Pounds								
+7								
+6								
+5								
+4								
+3								
+2								
+1								
Ideal weight								
−1								
−2								
−3								
−4								
−5								
−6								
−7								
WEIGHT								
Bust/chest								
Waist								
Hips								
Upper arms								
Thighs								
Period?								
WEEK								

Cambridge Weight Maintenance Chart

Pounds								
+7								
+6								
+5								
+4								
+3								
+2								
+1								
Ideal weight								
−1								
−2								
−3								
−4								
−5								
−6								
−7								
WEIGHT								
Bust/chest								
Waist								
Hips								
Upper arms								
Thighs								
Period?								
WEEK								

Cambridge Weight Maintenance Chart

Pounds								
+7								
+6								
+5								
+4								
+3								
+2								
+1								
Ideal weight								
−1								
−2								
−3								
−4								
−5								
−6								
−7								
WEIGHT								
Bust/chest								
Waist								
Hips								
Upper arms								
Thighs								
Period?								
WEEK								

Cambridge Weight Maintenance Chart

Pounds								
+7								
+6								
+5								
+4								
+3								
+2								
+1								
Ideal weight								
−1								
−2								
−3								
−4								
−5								
−6								
−7								
WEIGHT								
Bust/chest								
Waist								
Hips								
Upper arms								
Thighs								
Period?								
WEEK								

Cambridge Weight Maintenance Chart

Pounds								
+7								
+6								
+5								
+4								
+3								
+2								
+1								
Ideal weight								
−1								
−2								
−3								
−4								
−5								
−6								
−7								
WEIGHT								
Bust/chest								
Waist								
Hips								
Upper arms								
Thighs								
Period?								
WEEK								

Cambridge Weight Maintenance Chart

Pounds								
+7								
+6								
+5								
+4								
+3								
+2								
+1								
Ideal weight								
−1								
−2								
−3								
−4								
−5								
−6								
−7								
WEIGHT								
Bust/chest								
Waist								
Hips								
Upper arms								
Thighs								
Period?								
WEEK								

CAMBRIDGE WEIGHT MAINTENANCE CHART

Pounds								
+7								
+6								
+5								
+4								
+3								
+2								
+1								
Ideal weight								
−1								
−2								
−3								
−4								
−5								
−6								
−7								
WEIGHT								
Bust/chest								
Waist								
Hips								
Upper arms								
Thighs								
Period?								
WEEK								

CAMBRIDGE WEIGHT MAINTENANCE CHART

Pounds								
+7								
+6								
+5								
+4								
+3								
+2								
+1								
Ideal weight								
−1								
−2								
−3								
−4								
−5								
−6								
−7								
WEIGHT								
Bust/chest								
Waist								
Hips								
Upper arms								
Thighs								
Period?								
WEEK								